American Blues, Jazz & Soul Food, 2nd Edition

Featuring

Atlanta, Memphis, New Orleans and Washington DC

RON RUDISON

authorHOUSE®

AuthorHouse™
1663 Liberty Drive
Bloomington, IN 47403
www.authorhouse.com
Phone: 1 (800) 839-8640

Cover By Marlene Saulsbury

Published by AuthorHouse 12/05/2016

ISBN: 978-1-5049-7525-4 (sc)
ISBN: 978-1-5049-7524-7 (hc)
ISBN: 978-1-5049-7523-0 (e)

Library of Congress Control Number: 2016901181

Print information available on the last page.

This book is printed on acid-free paper.

Acknowledgments: In memory of my father, Raymond Dorest, New Orleans, LA jazz pianist and teacher, and my mother, Ollie Rudison Trim, Livingston Parish, LA teacher; dedicated to my children, Alexander, Andrea and Jodi. A special thanks to Col. Larry Thomas (USA Ret), Tony Duthie, Giles OKeeffe, James McGeady and Cynthia Lion for their creative input; saluting an inspiring entrepreneur, Kompari Rudison, Chief Executive Officer, Black Grove 401 Records, LLC.

TABLE OF CONTENTS

Visit our Website for important updates regarding Featured Venues: www.bluesjazzandsoulfood.com

Follow us on:
Facebook: American Blues, Jazz & Soul Food; www.youtube.com/bluesjazzandsoulfood and www.twitter.com/abjsf

PREFACE

I wrote "Where to Find the Best Soul Food, Blues and Jazz in the Southeast" in 1994. *American Blues, Jazz & Soul Food, 2nd Edition,* is an update of this guide and more. It is a celebration of three art forms that are unique to America. It also honors entrepreneurs that have nourished these art forms by providing outstanding venues in which the blues, jazz and soul food could be presented to the public. From a historical standpoint, the origins of blues, jazz and soul food should be viewed in context. While W.C. Handy, Buddy Boldin and the matrons of early soul food kitchens were developing and refining their arts in the early 20th century, visionaries such as Robert R. Church, Sr. were creating incredible venues in which the likes of W.C. Handy could showcase his enormous talent on Beale Street. By creating one of the South's first African American banks, Church also was able to rescue the historic Beale Street Baptist Church, an important institution in the social fabric of early Memphis life, from financial peril. In New Orleans, P.B.S. Pinchback was parlaying his substantial political influence into the creation of the landmark Southern University, also an important institution in the life of African Americans in New Orleans and Louisiana from the late 1800s forward. To really love and understand blues, jazz and soul food, it is important to understand and appreciate the prevailing culture from which they emerged.

INTRODUCTION

The soul food restaurant occupies a very special place in African American culture. Traditionally, the term "soul food" brings to mind a meal consisting of an entrée such as chitterlings with side dishes of greens—either collard, mustard, or turnip—and rice and candied yams, and corn bread. The term "soul food restaurant" embodies a cultural institution, a place where African Americans have traditionally come together after church, after work, or even after an evening out. The best soul food restaurants have always been important anchors within their respective communities, and for this reason, the establishments in this book have been selected as much for their cultural ambiance as for the quality of their food and the selections on their menus. Accordingly, traditional soul food restaurants—as well as those specializing in southern and Creole cuisine, barbecue and fish—are included.

African slaves brought many skills with them on their unwilling journey to America. Their knowledge of woodworking and metallurgy served their masters well during slavery. After they gained their freedom, these same skills enabled many to enter the trades as craftsmen. Slaves also came to America with the syncopated rhythms and melodies of Africa. They merged these with the European adaptations of the plantation owners and created a new music, a music that evolved from field chants to spirituals to ragtime and ultimately to blues, jazz, and gospel. African American cuisine evolved in a similar fashion. The slaves brought to the Americas a knowledge of spices and herbaceous roots, as well as recipes for transforming even the gamiest meats into culinary works of art. Add this to the lush vegetables, fruits, and grains of the Native Americans and the livestock introduced by planters and plantation owners, and you have the basic scenario for the evolution of soul food.

In effect, the two living conditions encountered by slaves in field quarters and in the "big house" resulted in the development of two separate, but related cuisines. The vast majority of slaves lived in field quarters and were more often than not given inferior cuts of meat: from the hog, entrails, feet, ears, and so on; from the chicken, wings, feet, gizzards, liver, and the like. As a means of economic necessity and survival, slave cooks adapted these coarse ingredients to sustain the field hands.

Meanwhile, slave cooks in the "big house" invariably worked with the choicest cuts of meat. They endeared themselves to all by emerging from the "plantation kitchen" with mouth-watering dishes such as smothered pork chops and steaks, beef stew, and fried, smothered or baked chicken accented by collard greens, corn bread and sweet potato pie. Ironically, the slave cook's magic with bitter greens made them irresistible to the residents of the plantation proper. When these plantation owners entertained guests from other parts of the country and abroad, their visitors must have been impressed by the fresh, robust, and exciting cuisine produced by the slave cooks. Imagine also their surprise when they heard the strange, syncopated new music emanating from the slave quarters.

Nowhere was this scene more often repeated than in the Mississippi Delta. The Mississippi Delta is a region along the border of Arkansas that ranges as far south as Vicksburg to just south of Memphis. To travel along Mississippi's Highway 61 is to retrace the history of the blues in America. New Orleans, Vicksburg, Rolling Fork, Greenville, Indianola, Cleveland, Clarksdale, and Tunica all parallel the highway that snakes along the border like its neighbor, the Mississippi River. At the turn of the 20th century, these Delta towns were the birthplace of many of America's blues legends. Son House, Mississippi John Hurt, Robert Johnson, Albert King, B.B. King, Memphis Minnie, McKinley Morganfield (Muddy Waters), Charlie Patton, and Bukka White are but a few from a very long list. Even before them, musicians were roaming the Delta, putting to music the hard conditions of life in the cotton fields that had their origins in slavery. This was a fertile environment for a young W.C. Handy to add form to the music, put it on paper, and share it with the rest of the United States and the world.

During the period when W.C. Handy was plying the Delta in search of the blues, Scott Joplin was refining another of America's original musical forms, ragtime. His syncopated piano style and numerous ragtime compositions earned him distinction as the king of rag. The emergence of blues and ragtime during the first decade of the 1900s captivated the entire country.

Also in the first decade of the century, a young cornet player in New Orleans named Buddy Bolden was taking a different direction. His improvisations on the cornet were mirrored by most of the young musicians of the city. Pianist Jelly Roll Morton and cornetist Joe "King" Oliver left New Orleans and took the music to Chicago, where, during the second decade of the century, jazz found a fertile environment and exploded across America. It also spread rapidly throughout Europe when Mobile, AL native James Reese took his 369th Infantry Division Band to Europe during World War I and brought African American music to a world stage.

Listen to Albert Collins's "Soul Food," James Arnold's "Red Beans and Rice" or Lou Rawls singing about "red beans and rice and candied yams" and you will get an idea about the relationship between the food and the music. As Charlie Davis of C. Davis Bar-B-Q in Houston puts it, "the barbecue and the blues just go together." So do jazz and Creole cuisine, according to Nina Buck of the chic Palm Court Jazz Café in New Orleans. Musicians and entertainers have always sought out soul food restaurants during their travels. In many ways, the music and the food are both defining elements of the people.

During the early 1940s and through the early 1950s, a period of American history when segregation was the rule, African American travel guides focused on three basic questions: Where can I stay? Where can I eat? And where can I go for entertainment? One such guide, *The Negro Green Book*, published in 1952, attempted to answer those questions in an ambitious project that covered cities across the country. One of the most interesting lists in this book cited the major African thoroughfares in each city. In a historical context, this list of famous streets chronicles the best of African American culture from the Harlem Renaissance of the 1920s through the mid-1960s. It also recalls what existed before single-family homeowners were displaced and their land was put to use for public projects such as interstate freeways. Huge, multifamily complexes replaced many private dwellings, and more affluent African Americans moved to the suburbs, setting the stage for the collapse of the inner cities in general, and these streets in particular. Many of the great theaters and soul food restaurants of the 1940s and 1950s also have been lost as a result. Some that have survived are highlighted in this book.

The international appeal of blues and jazz is well documented. In fact, blues and jazz artists historically have found their most appreciative audiences in Europe, Asia and South America. The appeal of soul food restaurants likewise crosses all cultural lines. Whether they are in Memphis, New Orleans, or Little Rock, their clientele typically represent all segments of their respective communities. The establishments included here are the best of the best.

ATLANTA

Atlanta is the cultural and financial center of the African American community in the Southeast and, many contend, the entire nation. Here, African American entrepreneurship is more than just a concept, it is an historical fact. Alonzo F. Herndon was one of Atlanta's first. Born a slave in 1858, he overcame those shackles and, in freedom, found an entrepreneurial niche as a barber. He opened several barber shops, invested in real estate, and became so successful that he amassed sufficient capital to found the Atlanta Life Insurance Company, one of the nation's most prosperous African American financial concerns. Herndon became one of Atlanta's wealthiest citizens during the early 1920s. Having accumulated great wealth, he also became a central figure in Atlanta education, community development and politics. His son, Norris, carried on that tradition. He and his father also were pioneering African American philanthropists. In 1928, former Morehouse College student William A. Scott II founded the Atlanta Daily World, America's first, successful African American Daily newspaper that continues in circulation today.

African American churches always have been at the center of African American life. Big Bethel African Methodist Episcopal Church was founded in 1847. According to church history, the first public school for African Americans in Atlanta, the Gate City Colored School, was organized in Big Bethel's basement in 1879. Before moving to its first campus, Morris Brown College also was nurtured in the church's basement in 1891. Ebenezer Baptist Church was founded in 1886. Ebenezer's first pastor was Rev. John A. Parker, a former slave. He was succeeded by Rev. Alfred Daniel Williams in 1894. Rev. Williams was an early leader in Atlanta's civil rights movement. His son-in-law, Rev. Martin Luther King, Sr. followed him in 1931 as pastor. Martin Luther King, Jr. joined his father as co-pastor in 1960. The rest is civil rights history.

The median standard of living for Atlanta's African American residents ranks among the country's highest. The broad economic base, plus a large number of registered minority voters, has translated into a broad political base. The late Maynard Jackson was elected the city's first African American mayor in 1974, serving until 1982, then again from 1990 to 1994. He was succeeded by Andrew Young after his second term in office in 1982. Before serving as mayor, Young helped lead the civil rights movement at Rev. Dr. Martin Luther King Jr.'s side during the 1960s, served as a U. S. Congressman from Georgia during the period 1973-1977, was appointed by former President Jimmy Carter as the nation's first African American ambassador to the United Nations in 1977, and was a key member of the committee that secured Atlanta as the host of the 1996 Olympics. Andrew Young's resume continues without peer in the city.

Political luminaries such as Julian Bond, the late Mary Young-Cummings (former Georgia state representative), and former mayor Shirley Franklin also have been among the city's preeminent leaders during modern times.

Atlanta's current and recent cadre of African American leadership is impressive, but there were many who paved the way before them. W.E.B. Du Bois, a man who fired political debate and cultural awareness throughout the African American populace, taught at Atlanta University for 13 years, beginning in the late 1890s. In 1884, poet/novelist/lawyer/U.S Consul James Weldon Johnson graduated from Atlanta University. Five years later, he wrote a poem entitled "Lift Every Voice and Sing." It was set to music by his brother, John Rosamond Johnson, and quickly became known as the African American National Anthem. Just over a half century later, it was to become the anthem of the civil rights movement. Atlanta native, the Rev. Dr. Martin Luther King Jr., captured the imaginations and hearts of the world while leading the Montgomery, AL bus boycott in 1963 and, from thereon, America's civil rights movement. Atlanta University and Clark College (Clark-Atlanta University by merger), Morehouse College, Spelman College, and Morris Brown University, have helped generations of African Americans develop their full potential. Distinguished graduates also include Moredcai Johnson (Morehouse 1911), Dr. Nathaniel H. Bronner, Sr., (Morehouse 1940), Rev. Dr. Martin Luther King, Jr. (Morehouse 1948), Lerone Bennett Jr. (Morehouse 1949), Dr. Juel Pate Borders (Spelman 1954), Maj. Gen. Marcelite Harris (Spelman 1964), Rev. Dr. Calvin O Butts, III (Morehouse 1972), Shelton Jackson "Spike" Lee (Morehouse

1979), and many other men and women who have left a profound and continuing legacy for the entire country.

Gertrude "Ma" Rainey, a native of Columbus, GA was one of the early women of the blues who took the music to new heights as a popular American art form. Born in 1886, her vocal range and flare for elaborate dress and costumes propelled her to widespread appeal across the south. Recording with the likes of Louis Armstrong and Coleman Hawkins, she gained immense popularity and can be said to have been one of America's earliest "Divas" in the history of jazz and blues. In fact, she is widely considered the "Mother of the Blues." Ma Rainey also mentored another blues legend, Chattanooga, Tennessee's Bessie Smith. They performed together during Bessie Smith's early teens; until Smith's talents soared beyond their collaboration and she went on to garner national and international acclaim as the "Empress of the Blues."

Blind Willie McTell (Thomson, GA), Eugene "Buddy" Moss (Jewell, GA), Robert Hicks (Walnut Gove, GA) and Thomas Andrew Dorsey (Villa Rica, GA) were among Atlanta's early blues legends. They all, including Bessie Smith, relocated to Atlanta during the early 1900s, drawn by the attraction of performing in venues on the city's historic Sweet Auburn Avenue. Dorsey achieved legendary status on a national stage and international stage. After writing and recording hundreds of blues songs, his blues gave way to something very precious. During a period of illness and despair, a song was placed on his heart, "Precious Lord, Take My Hand." He teamed with another gospel pioneer, Mahalia Jackson, and became recognized in American music history as the father of gospel music.

Many consider Atlanta to be the crown jewel of the South. The city's cultural attractions and entertainment options are impressive, making it a "must visit" on any trip through America's South.

JAZZ/BLUES/REGGAE:

Blind Willie's

Location: 828 N Highland Ave
Telephone: (404) 873-BLUE
Clientele: Young/Mature Adult
Format: Blues
Calendar: Live Entertainment Mon - Sat
Cover/Minimum: Yes/No
Dress: Casual/Classy
URL: www.blindwilliesblues.com

Comments: Named after Atlanta's most renowned blues star, "Blind Willie" McTell, Blind Willie's looks and feels like everything a blues club should be. The building dates back to the 1920s or 1930s, and the club is a cozy rectangular room with high ceilings and low lights. The bricks and floor are original. Most of the seating is snug up against the stage, with a few tables located across from the sit-down bar in the rear of the room; all seats give an unobstructed view of the performers. Eric King and his partner, Roger Gregory, founded the club in 1986. King had long hosted his own blues show on WRFG-FM (89.3) radio, and he knew what Atlantans wanted. Although Blind Willie's started out on a shoestring budget, it had a good nucleus of local blues artists who were starving for exposure, and the club has since become the city's foremost venue for launching the careers of its native talents. Some of the most popular acts that have been featured here include Luther "Houserocker" Johnson (regularly appearing with the Shadows, the club's house band), Sandra Hall, and Lotsa Poppa. Poppa often toured with legendary R&B crooners Jerry Butler, Sam Cooke, and Jackie Wilson during the 1960s and was a regular feature at Atlanta's famed Royal Peacock Club. The partners also brought in national touring acts, mostly friends they had met at events such as the annual New Orleans Jazz & Heritage Blues Festival. Atlantans have really taken to this establishment, and rightfully so. It's a place where you can hear the New Orleans-flavored blues of the Roulettes on one evening, the Texas-style blues of Johnny Copeland on another and the Delta influences of the legendary Dave "Honeyboy" Edwards on yet another. Blind Willie's also provides a menu that is sure to please. Try their New Orleans style jambalaya, Memphis-influenced BBQ pork sandwich or Chicago dog, described as "a classic Vienna Jumbo Dog served with mustard onion, tomato, relish, pickle, sport peppers and celery salt." King, who considers himself a blues buff almost from birth, and blues sideman Gregory have long nurtured a love affair with this American art form, and as a result, they have given the city of Atlanta a great treasure, a venue where you can hear outstanding local, regional and national blues artists.

JAZZ/BLUES/REGGAE:

Café 290

Location: 290 Hilderbrand Dr NE, Sandy Springs, GA
Telephone: (404) 256-3942
Clientele: Young/Mature Adult
Format: Jazz, R&B
Calendar: Live Entertainment Tues – Sat, Some Sundays
Cover/Minimum: Yes/Yes
Dress: Classy
URL: www.cafe290atlanta.com

Comments: Owner John Scatena's goal is to present Atlanta area citizens with a venue that will evolve into the regions' preeminent jazz venue. The club has enjoyed enormous popularity, attracting patrons from throughout the Metro Atlanta Area and celebrities from far and near. Café 290 is tastefully appointed, softly lit and cozy. Paintings of jazz greats such as Louis Armstrong, Billie Holiday and Duke Ellington are arrayed throughout the dining room, compliments of artists William Floyd and Najee respectively. Trumpeter/vocalist Joe Gransden and his big band perform each first and third Monday evening. Saxophonist Gary Harris hosts a very popular jam session on Sunday evenings. Scatena proudly states that these sessions have led to the discovery of local talent by actor/director/playwright Tyler Perry; he has featured some local artists on television productions and movies. Café 290's entertainment lineup varies most other nights. Celebrities who claim this venue among their favorites include Tyler Perry, actors and comedians Jamie Foxx and Chris Tucker, actor/producer/comedian David Chapelle, Grammy Award-winning record producer/songwriter L.A. Reid and Tony Award winning actress/singer Jennifer Holiday. Located just a few minutes north of Atlanta's Buckhead District, a visit to Café 290 will definitely be among one of the highlights of any visit to Atlanta.

JAZZ/BLUES/REGGAE:

Churchill Grounds Jazz Café

Location: 660 Peachtree St. NE
Telephone: (404-876-3030)
Clientele: Young/Mature Adult
Format: Jazz
Calendar: Live Entertainment Tues – Sat, Some Sundays
Cover/Minimum: Yes/Yes
Dress: Classy
URL: www.churchillgrounds.com

Comments: Churchill Grounds Jazz Café has seized the mantle as Atlanta's most important and consistent jazz club. The club has a commitment to bringing in top regional and national artists while also providing a platform for growing the next generation of jazz greats. Composer, educator and drummer Justin Chesarek and his quintet are featured on Wednesday nights. The focus of Chesarek's Quintet is modern jazz, playing their original compositions and nudging their audience towards an appreciation for the future of jazz. They do it well. Recent artists have included drummer Bernard Linnette and his quartet playing straight ahead, Latin and avant garde, soul cycle with their exciting blend of jazz, hip-hop, R&B and world music as well as vocalist and trumpet player Joe Gransden. Gransden held his record release party and performance here for his album, Live At Churchill Grounds. I took in a show by saxophonist Jacques Schwarz-Bart during my first visit.

Accompanied by vocalist Stephanie McKay, pianist Milan Milanovich, drummer Chris Burris and Joel Powell on bass guitar, the quartet delivered a performance that was scintillating. The improvisations and interplay between Schwarz-Bart and McKay were, in some moments, electric and intimate. At one point the audience glimpsed an intimacy that was so profound that one had the illusion of overhearing a conversation between two lovers. They are, after all, husband and wife. The quartet took the audience on a musical journey via modern jazz with hints of bebop and Afro-Caribbean flavors. Jacques Schwarz-Bart counts among his tonal influences John Coltrane and Coleman Hawkins. His style embraces his native gwo ka folk music tradition (Guadeloupe), soul music and modern jazz. Churchill Grounds' owner, Sam Yi, is an avid jazz connoisseur. He developed his love of the genre from his mother who constantly played jazz in their home when he was a child in Seoul, Korea. Yi considers it his duty to honor the jazz medium, the musicians who perform the art and the public who support and love jazz. The success of this 13-year club is unarguable. Voted top jazz venue in Atlanta by Atlanta Magazine and Creating Loafing Atlanta on numerous occasions, Churchill Grounds Jazz Café also has been acclaimed one of the top 100 jazz clubs in the world by Down Beat's International Jazz Guide.

JAZZ/BLUES/REGGAE:

Dante's Down the Hatch

Location: 3380 Peachtree Rd. NE
Telephone: (404) 266-1600/577-1800
Clientele: Young/Mature Adult
Format: Jazz
Calendar: Live Entertainment Nightly
Cover/Minimum: Yes/Yes
Dress: Classy
URL: www.dantesdownthehatch.com

Comments: Dante Stephensen always has been a man of entrepreneurial vision, from the days of his childhood lemonade stands and newspaper routes. His tour in the Navy as a member of the underwater demolition team and later as a founding member of the Navy's elite SEAL team, and his service in Vietnam forged in him the discipline and toughness to stay true to that vision. Paul F. Mitchell, a longtime fixture in Atlanta's jazz scene, recalled meeting Stephensen when he performed at Atlanta's Playboy Club in the mid-1960s. They hit it off and Stephensen said that he wanted to open a jazz supper club. Mitchell responded that he would gladly play his venue. Stephensen founded Dante's in 1970 in Underground Atlanta. True to his word, the Paul F. Mitchell Trio was the feature act from the very beginning, and their music achieved an enormous following throughout the region and nationally. The club lasted until 1981 when the Underground Atlanta Corporation closed. Stephensen built another, larger version of the club in Buckhead in 1981. His original Down the Hatch was reopened in 1989 with the revival of Underground Atlanta, but again closed. Dante's boasts a format you are not likely to find at any other venue: fine dining and elegant jazz, both showcased in a setting that gives the illusion of an 18th-century sailing vessel tied to the docks of a Mediterranean Sea village. When you walk across the "moat" into the club, you can observe live crocodiles, all securely lodged in a confined area below, of course! I counted six. Seated at a table on the second floor, I had the sensation of being in a low-slung crow's nest with the band only a few feet away.

The Paul Mitchell Trio played Dante's for 30 years, until Mitchell passed away in 2000. His protégé, Morris Brown College graduate John Robertson, has taken the mantle and upholds the tradition started by Mitchell. He has been playing the room for over 10 years. He and his trio previously played at the old Underground Atlanta location for 5 years. With Edwin Williams on upright, Terry Smith on drums and vocalist Rosemary Rainey, the trio delights audiences with a wide range of jazz that is just the ticket for a romantic evening in a delightful environment. Everyone's been here, from former Presidents Jimmy Carter and George Bush to entertainment giants Charlton Heston and Gladys Knight. This is simply a must-stop when visiting Atlanta!

JAZZ/BLUES/REGGAE:

Fat Matt's

Location: 1811 Piedmont Ave., NE
Telephone: (404) 607-1622
Clientele: Young/Mature Adult
Format: Blues
Calendar: Live Entertainment Nightly
Cover/Minimum: No/No
Dress: Casual
URL: www.fatmattsribshack.com

Comments: Fat Matt's is both a rib house and a blues joint. It's more like a trendy suburban café than like the down-home places you would find along the Mississippi Delta, but the atmosphere is still laid-back. Some patrons enter and head straight for the counter on the right, where you can see the barbecue fire going and the meat being prepared. Others grab one of the 45 or so seats inside, all scattered about tables that place the stage in easy view. Or they opt for one of the booths on the adjoining patio that also provide good vantage points for hearing and seeing the band. Life-long blues lover Matt Harper opened Fat Matt's in September 1990, and after a lean first six months, the business really took off. The long lines on most weekends attest to a formula that works: good local blues and good barbecue.

You can hear Little Brother on Sunday, the Lee Griffin Band on Monday, Rough Draft on Tuesday, open mike night on Wednesday, Chicken Shack featuring Felix Reyes on Thursday, and a revolving selection of hot local bands on Friday and Saturday. Jimmy Rodgers, Jr. sat in on one of their open mike nights. Buster Poindexter and Emilio Estevez stopped by when they were filming the movie *Free Jack.* So did former football star Dick Butkus for a "record amount of ribs" during the 1994 Super Bowl. The ribs are among the tenderest available anywhere and the barbecue chicken first-rate. Don't mind if you see a line when you drive up – it moves quickly. Besides, you're bound to agree that a generous portion of succulent ribs and hot blues make the wait well worthwhile.

JAZZ/BLUES/REGGAE:

Maddy's Rib & Blues Joint

Location: 1479 Scott Blvd, Decatur, GA
Telephone: (404) 377-0301
Clientele: Young/Mature Adult
Format: Blues
Calendar: Live Entertainment Tues - Sun
Cover/Minimum: Yes/No
Dress: Casual
Status: CLOSED

Comments: Maddy's offers great ribs, either by the slab, half slab or sandwich, quarter or half chicken and all the sides and fixin's. This cozy club also serves up great blues. You can catch the Denton Perry Blues Ensemble on Tuesdays, the Blues Barons on Wednesdays, an open jam hosted by Chicago Joe Jones on Thursdays and JT Speed most Sundays. On my first visit one Thursday evening, I was surprised to find a group of youngsters on stage, ranging in age from 10 to 15. Some were Joe Jones' students; others came from locales throughout the Atlanta metro area. They all had one thing in common, prodigious talent. Maddy's and Joe Jones have hit upon a great concept: provide a venue that features the next generation of blues artist and let them grow. According to Georgia Tech Professor Dr. William D. Hunt, it is a welcome opportunity to immerse his young son in an art form that he is beginning to find very compelling. Dr. Hunt was one of several parents in the audience who proudly watched and listened to their kids take flight, encouraged by the hours of practice and the results unfolding before their very eyes. Washington DC's House of Blues features a similar, but broader concept for high school jazz students, a concept that is essential for keeping these art forms alive. Stop by Maddy's Rib & Blues Joint for outstanding local acts and the next generation of blues legends in the making.

JAZZ/BLUES/REGGAE:

Northside Tavern

Location: 1058 Howell Mill RD NW
Telephone: (404) 874-8745
Clientele: Young/Mature Adult
Format: Blues
Calendar: Live Entertainment Nightly
Cover/Minimum: Yes/No
Dress: Casual
URL: www.northsidetavern.com

Comments: The Northside Tavern occupies a building that was constructed the 1940s. It opened as a grocery store then became a package store and ultimately a bar. It was purchased by the late Butler Webb, who operated the bar from 1969 until his passing in 1989. His daughter, Ella Webb, has been the sole proprietor since her father's death. Local musician Danny "Mudcat" Deudeck approached Ella with a concept for a blues venue in 1992 and the club has quickly evolved, becoming a force on the Atlanta blues scene. It is considered by many as one of Atlanta's best "blues juke joints." A stellar lineup of local, regional and national acts has performed here. Among their most notable were Jamaica-born and Dothan, AL-raised Eddie Kirkland, a legendary guitarist, harp player and singer who spent over a decade playing with John Lee Hooker; the late guitarist/ vocalist Cora Mae Bryant, a third-generation Georgia Blues pioneer in the tradition of her grandmother, Savanna "Dip" Weaver and her father, Curley James Weaver; Macon, GA native Robert Lee Coleman; Nashville, TN-based Uncle Sugar; and Atlanta-based Beverly "Guitar" Watson, a septuagenarian who still is bringing it strong. Northside Tavern is a true blues joint that ranks high on the list of must-visits when you are in Atlanta and craving for some down-home blues.

JAZZ/BLUES/REGGAE:

Ray's In the City

Location: 240 Peachtree Street NW
Telephone: (404) 524-9224
Clientele: Young/Mature Adult
Format: Jazz, Classical, Rock…
Calendar: Live Entertainment Thur - Sat
Cover/Minimum: No/No
Dress: Classy
URL: www.raysrestaurants.com

Comments: Ray's In the City is a beautiful supper club located in the heart of downtown Atlanta. Their music calendar ranges from rock to classical to jazz. Their jazz lineup features local artist such as vocalist Kayla Taylor with acoustic guitarist Steve Moore, vocalist Valerie Hines, and pianist/vocalist Rich Rowlinson. Their menu features a tantalizing array of seafood that includes blackened mahi mahi Alexander, horseradish crusted grouper, shrimp and crawfish étouffée and sun corn-crusted Georgia mountain trout and more. The ownership group of Ray's In the City also have unveiled two other restaurants in their impressive portfolio, Ray's On the River at 6700 Powers Ferry Road, Sandy Springs, GA and Ray's Killer Creek at 1700 Mansell Road (at Georgia 400) in Alpharetta, GA. Each represents top-flight dining and entertainment options when visiting the Atlanta area.

JAZZ/BLUES/REGGAE:

The Royal Peacock

Location: 186 Auburn Ave, NE
Telephone: (404) 880-0745
Clientele: Young Adult
Format: Reggae/Calypso
Calendar: Live Entertainment varies
Cover/Minimum: Yes/No
Dress: Casual / Classy
URL: www.theroyalpeacock.com

Comments: Carrie Cunningham purchased the Top Hat Club in 1949 and renamed it the Royal Peacock. She also owned the Royal Hotel on "Sweet Auburn Avenue," having purchased it in 1937. One of Cunningham's first acts upon purchasing the old Top Hat was to transform it into an even more exquisite venue, peacock feathers and all. In the 1950s and 1960s, The Royal Peacock was the place to go in downtown Atlanta for African American entertainment. It was a stylish showcase for top R&B blues, and jazz acts – if you could play The Royal Peacock, your next stop had to be the fabled Apollo in New York City. Mention the Peacock to longtime residents of Atlanta, and the stories start to flow. Dorothy Clements, owner of the Auburn Avenue Rib Shack, recalls legendary performances by artists such as jazz vocalist Cab Calloway, Nat King Cole, and

Nina Simone. Doug Berry, maintenance technician for the Chit-Chat Restaurant & Lounge, says that he used to slip into the Peacock as a teenager and take in great R&B acts such as Bobby "Blues" Bland, Clarence Carter, Sam Cooke, Johnnie Taylor, and Jackie Wilson. Blues legends such as "Muddy Waters," "Howlin' Wolf," B.B. King, Ben E. King and jazz greats Miles Davis and Dizzy Gillespie all made their way here. In a recent article featured in the Georgia Music Magazine, Delois Scott, granddaughter of Carrie Cunningham is quoted as saying, "Everybody calls the Royal Peacock the 'incubator' for artists. When Little Richard first started playing here, he was an unknown. When Ray Charles was first starting an unknown, he played here, James Brown, unknown. Gladys and the Pips, unknown. Nat King Cole played here before he even started singing..." The Royal Peacock has gone through a number of makeovers since those storied years, but remains an historic venue on "Sweet Auburn Avenue." It has re-emerged as a reggae and rap venue, still playing host to those who would "make it big." Their website boasts that "Young Jock signed a deal w\ Bad Boy South," a reference to Yung Joc's bio where he recalls performing his mixtape, *It's Goin' Down, live at the Peacock in 2005 where he was discovered by* Russell "Block" Spencer of Block Entertainment. This led to him signing a record deal with Block's Entertainment label in collaboration with Sean Comb's Bad Boy South label. The Royal Peacock usually hosts a rap talent showcase on Wednesday nights and features reggae music most Saturday nights.

DINING:

Busy Bee

Location: 810 Martin Luther King Dr. SW
Telephone: (404) 525-9212
Proprietor: Tracy A. Gates
Dress: Casual
Menu: Soul Food, Southern Cuisine
Price: Modest
Hours: Mon – Fri 11:00 AM to 7:00 PM; Sun Noon to 7:00 PM
URL: www.thebusybeecafe.com

Comment: Busy Bee was founded in 1947. Needless to say, it is a landmark eatery with tons of tradition. I recall eating great meals here during the late 1960s while studying at nearby Morehouse College. It was a cozy stop where you could get down-home cooking and be reminded of meals cooked by mom. It remains a favorite stop for students, local residents and visitors from across the country. The exterior of the restaurant is very modest. Once inside, a cozy ambiance invites sit down dining or carryout. Menu items include soul food staples such as chittlins, giblets, ham hocks, neck bones and fried or smothered chicken. Veggies range from broccoli cheese casserole to baby lima beans. You also will want to try desserts such as their very popular banana pudding or red velvet cake. The restaurant is located adjacent the historic Pasqual's Hotel & Restaurant which now is owned by Clark-Atlanta University. Stop by Busy Bee and experience history while enjoying delicious soul food.

DINING:

Gladys Knight and Ron Winans' Chicken & Waffles

Location: 529 Peachtree St NE
Telephone: (404) 874-9393
Proprietor: Gladys Knight and Ron Winans
Dress: Casual/Classy
Menu: Soul Food
Price: Moderate
Hours: Mon-Thu 11am-11pm; Fri-Sat 11am-4am; Sun 11am-8pm
URL: www.gladysandron.net

Comments: A Harlem tradition comes to Atlanta: Wells Restaurant introduced Harlem to chicken & waffles at the height of the Harlem Renaissance. Gladys Knight, her son Shanga Hankerson, and Ron Winans have created Gladys Knight and Ron Winans' Chicken and Waffles and introduced the concept to an appreciative Atlanta community.

The décor of the restaurant is elegant; the ambiance radiates the comfortable feel of both a dining room and a living room. Soft leather seats, mahogany wood panels and posts along with soothing R&B music piped over the room provide just the right touch. Photos of celebrity guests line the walls. Here and there, you can view displays of Gladys' Grammy winning albums, a pair of stiletto heels from a concert long ago and a full-length portrait from one of her memorable concerts. Their menu features a wide range of soul food, Southern and vegetarian cuisine. Most come for their signature chicken & waffles. I tried the shrimp sauté with zucchini, mushrooms, squash, broccoli and green peppers, all nestled on a bed of white rice. It was an exquisite meal. You also may want to try their smothered chicken, brown sugar salmon, shrimp & grits or veggie soul, a smorgasbord that consists of your choice of up to four veggie dishes such as squash casserole, collard greens, black eyed peas, rice & gravy or candied yams. If you still have room for more, go all out and try something really decadent, say a slice of sweet potato cheesecake or peach cobbler, sinfully topped with a scoop of vanilla ice cream.

Get there early, but prepare to stand in line a bit. Patrons begin to cue up from the moment the restaurant opens. Some come because they've heard the rave reviews, others come because they've "been there, done that," and are coming back for more. I'll be back, and so should you.

DINING:

Justin's Restaurant & Bar

Location: 2200 Peachtree Rd. NE
Telephone: (404) 603-5353
Proprietor: Sean "Diddy" Combs
Dress: Classy
Menu: Southern & Caribbean Cuisine
Price: Moderate / Expensive
Hours: Sun-Thurs 5:00 PM -11:00 PM, Fri & Sat 5 PM – Midnight; Sun Brunch 11:00 AM - 3 PM
Status: CLOSED

Comments: Great cuisine, ambiance and entertainment. Justin's is one of Atlanta's most popular venues to see and be seen. From the moment that you drive up, you know that this is a new age venue serving the city's younger generation of movers and shakers. An interior that is equally bold and modern accentuates this theme. So does the hip hop music that is piped throughout the room. Owner Sean Combs is an American success story. He has parlayed a work ethic that can be characterized as old school into a multi-million dollar entertainment empire. From his Harlem birth in 1969 to a two-year stint at Howard University in 1988 to an internship at New York-based Uptown Records in 1990, Combs' rise to fame and fortune has been meteoric. He has overcome some road blocks along the way; however, the lesson for all, both young and old, is this: don't let your road blocks and adversity become mountains, but rather, stepping stones to higher achievement. P-Diddy certainly has done this and more. His career as founder of Bad Boy Entertainment, record company executive, rapper, producer, men's clothier and entrepreneur has catapulted him to the top of the hip hop industry and culture. Sean Combs opened his first restaurant, Justin's in New York City in 1997. He followed that with the opening of Justin's in Atlanta in 1998. Justin's is named for Combs' son, Justin, and inspired by and dedicated to his grandmother, Jesse Smalls. The restaurant's menu features Caribbean inspired treats such as chicken curry and calypso chicken, Creole-inspired Cornish hen jambalaya, stuffed blackened catfish (catfish filet stuffed with crab meat shrimp and three peppers) and soulful cuisine such as smothered turkey wings, fried chicken and side veggies that include red beans & rice, collard greens, candied yams and steamed cabbage.

DINING:

Paschal's Restaurant

Location: 180-B Northside Dr.
Telephone: (404) 525-2023
Proprietor: James Paschal and Herman J. Russell
Dress: Classy
Menu: Southern Cuisine
Price: Moderate - Expensive
Hours: Mon – Sat: 11:00 AM – 9:00 PM, Sunday Brunch: 11:00 Am – 4:00 PM
Sunday Dinner: 4:00 PM – 9:00 PM
URL: www.paschalsatlanta.com

Comments: The new Paschal's Restaurant was founded in 2002 by two Atlanta icons, hotelier and restaurateur James Paschal and real estate entrepreneur Herman J. Russell.

Their venture is bold and exciting. The reclamation of a historic concept is an enormous gift to the city and the citizens of Atlanta. The contributions of the Paschal brothers and Herman Russell to the history and growth of Atlanta are well documented. The forerunner of the new Paschal's Restaurant, Paschal's Hotel and Restaurant, was a landmark institution, reserving a special place in the history of Civil Rights movement. The current restaurant manager, Marshall Slack, served as a manager for the original Paschal's for over 30 years. He witnessed firsthand the power breakfasts where the Rev. Dr. Martin Luther, Jr. and his associates Rev. Andrew Young, Rev. Joseph Lowery, Rev. Ralph David Abernathy and others chartered the course of the nation's Civil Rights movement. Students from the colleges of Clark, Morehouse, and Morris Brown and Atlanta University would use the hotel as a headquarters when they returned from protest marches and sit-ins, sharing their stories of arrest and intimidation with parents in the restaurant and hotel lobby. Slack also helped the Paschal brothers book and plan logistics for legendary entertainers who played the hotel's La Carousel Club; the likes of Ramsey Lewis, Cannonball Adderly, Lou Rawls, Aretha Franklin and the Modern Jazz Quartet, to name a few. After taking a hiatus from the hospitality industry following the sale of Paschal's Hotel and Restaurant to Clark-Atlanta University in1996, Marshall Slack was persuaded to return for the opening of the new Paschal's Restaurant by James Paschal. Mr. Paschal's rationale? "We need you—besides, you still owe me money." With that, the soft-spoken Slack laughed and was reunited with his friend, James Paschal. He has brought old-fashioned management skills to a new generation of staff, from the kitchen to the dining room to the hosts and hostesses who greet guests upon arriving.

The restaurant's menu is highlighted by the fried chicken recipe that has endeared the restaurant to patrons from across America for more than half a century. My order was as delicious as my first meal at Paschal's while a student at Morehouse in 1968. You can order fried or roasted chicken by halves or quarters. Home-style pot roast, blackened catfish, Castleberry Hill shrimp and grits, braised short ribs, assorted steaks, and pastas round out the menu choices. As an exclamation point, try their soulful vegetable sides such as collard greens, fried okra, steamed broccoli or candied yams. Be sure to save room for one of their irresistible desserts: peach cobbler, bourbon pecan pie, or New Orleans-style bread pudding with rum sauce. The new Paschal's Restaurant should be highlighted on your itinerary when visiting Atlanta. It is located near the Atlanta University Center, just a 10 minute walk to the Georgia Dome.

DINING:

The Beautiful Restaurant

Location: 2260 Cascade Road
Telephone: (404) 752-5931
Proprietor: The Perfect Church
Dress: Casual / Classy
Menu: Soul Food/Southern
Price: Very Modest
Hours: Daily: 7:00 a.m. – 11:00 p.m.
http:// www.beautifulrestaurant-atlanta.com

Comments: The Beautiful Restaurant is one of Atlanta's finest for soul food and Southern cuisine. The Perfect Church, a Holiness congregation, opened their initial restaurant in 1979. They have owned five restaurants over the years, but have settled on one, their original Beautiful Restaurant at the Cascade location in southwest Atlanta. The church started their first eating establishment because they wanted a place where congregation members could get fresh vegetables cooked in all natural oils, without pork. It was an immediate success. The Beautiful Restaurants are perfect examples of economic empowerment, and their delicious meals are a fantastic value. Many Atlanta natives come here for the restaurants' vegetable platter (three veggies, cornbread, and a beverage for $3.19!), but I couldn't resist the baked Cornish hen, rice pilaf, and collard greens. I had my entree at the Auburn Avenue restaurant and saved room for dessert at the Cascade location. There Mrs. Lenora Reese, general manager, surprised me with three different desserts: peach cobbler, apple cobbler, and banana pudding. They were all delicious beyond words. Other items on the menu include braised short ribs, T-bone steaks, chicken flavored rice, squash and green beans. The ambiance of the restaurant is enhanced by numerous potted plants and a meticulously landscaped lawn. A display case houses fresh homemade apple and carrot juice along with garden salads. The décor is alive with hues of gold, orange, and white. The Beautiful Restaurant is a great choice when considering your dining options in Atlanta.

DINING:

Thelma's Kitchen

Location: 302 Auburn Ave.
Telephone: (404) 688-5855
Proprietor: Thelma Grundy
Dress: Casual
Menu: Southern
Price: Very Modest
Hours: Mon – Fri, 7:30AM – 4:30PM

Comments: Ambiance and chic dining are not the order of the day here – just down-home cooking at its finest! A small serving line up front has a display case where featuring piping hot entrees such as country-fried steak, barbecue chicken, roast beef, baked ham, and okra cakes. The room seats about 70. It's a good thing, too, because around noon the restaurant is teeming with patrons from the downtown business district. Thelma Grundy started out with a hot dog stand in the early 1960s, and she has owned restaurants in different locations throughout the city ever since. In recent years, she has established quite a following in her Luckie Street location. Each member of her family has lent a hand. Thelma's husband Riley recently came in to help oversee the business after retiring from 35 years of service with a local printing company. David and Joseph Grundy alternate with their mother as chefs in the kitchen. Thelma's is not only a staple for Atlanta's business community, but also a favorite among local sports figures as well. Atlanta Braves star David Justice is one of her most loyal customers. Heavyweight boxing champion Evander Holyfield is a regular. When Atlanta Hawks journeyman player Enis Whatley stopped by to chat during my interview with Mrs. Grundy, he indicated that he eats all of his pregame meals here. Grits and eggs with either salmon cakes or sausage were the most-requested breakfast entrees. The fried chicken is crisp on the outside, moist and tender inside. Thelma's now has relocated to the site of the former Auburn Avenue Rib Shack, a welcome revival of this historic venue that was once a favorite venue for many of Atlanta's civil rights leaders during the 1960s.

Atlanta Walk About

Martin Luther King Jr. Historical Site

Ghandi Statue at the Martin Luther King Jr. Historical Site

Birth Home at the Martin Luther King Jr. Historical Site

Harkness Hall at historic Morehouse College

← Spelman College

MORRIS
BROWN
COLLEGE
FOUNDED 1881

Ray Charles Center for the Performing Arts

MEMPHIS, TENNESSEE

One of the founding fathers of Memphis was Andrew Jackson, who was later to become the United States' seventh president. Jackson's longtime friend and real estate partner, John Overton, purchased huge parcels of land on the banks of the Mississippi and Wolf Rivers in the 1780s, then sold half his share to Andrew Jackson. Six years later, Jackson sold half of his share to James Winchester. In 1818, Andrew Jackson and Isaac Shelby were appointed to a commission by President James Monroe to negotiate the purchase of lands held by the Chickasaw Indians. The resulting treaty and purchase netted the U.S. government 6.8 million acres of land along the western Tennessee and northern Mississippi borders, thus laying the foundation for what was to grow into one of the South's jewel cities, Memphis, TN.

Two events that have had a profound effect on the character of American life took place here. In 1968, the Reverend Martin Luther King, Jr., came to the city to show support for the striking Memphis sanitation workers. It was during this visit that he was assassinated while standing on the balcony of the Lorraine Motel. This single moment crystallized the civil rights movement in the United States. It gave added momentum to the struggle for civil and human rights, elevated the consciousness of all Americans, and assured Rev. Dr. King an immortal place worldwide as a champion of freedom.

The Windsor Hotel originally was constructed circa 1925. It was purchased in 1942 by an African American businessman, Walter Bailey. He renamed it the Lorraine, a testament to his wife Loree, and the jazz standard made famous by Nat King Cole in the early 1940s, "Sweet Lorraine." The Lorraine was expanded over the years, eventually becoming the Lorraine Motel. It emerged as an important adjunct to the "Chittlin Circuit," a welcome source of lodging and food for African American visitors to Memphis during the 1940s, '50s and '60s. Legendary entertainers such as Louis Armstrong, Nat King Cole, Sarah Vaughan and Ray Charles, were among their distinguished register of guests. So was Rev. Dr. Martin Luther King Jr. during a visit in support of the Memphis Sanitation workers in March 1968. He stayed there yet again in April 1968 while visiting to organize a follow-up demonstration supporting the Sanitation Workers. On April 3, 1968, Dr. King gave his historic "I've Been to the Mountain Top" speech at the Memphis Mason Temple. He was assassinated the following evening on that fateful balcony that has been stenciled upon the consciousness of American History. Walter Bailey's wife, Loree, was taken ill within hours of Dr. King's death, and passed away a day later. Over the years, Bailey was to maintain Room 306 and the accompanying 307 as memorials to both Dr. King and his wife. The Lorraine began to decline in the wake of the tragedy, so much so that it ended up at auction "on the courthouse steps," only to be rescued by concerned Memphis businessmen. The State of Tennessee, Shelby County and the Memphis City government provided $8 million in funding to make the vision of the late owner, Walter Bailey, a reality. It opened in 1992 as the National Civil Rights Museum.

The National Civil Rights Museum

The second event occurred more than half a century earlier when William Christopher Handy reached down into the depths of his soul, tapped into the trials and tribulations of "Negro folk," and came up with a rhythm that is uniquely American: the blues. Like a number of the great artists in African American history, Handy came from a line of preachers. He was born in Florence, AL on November 16, 1873 in a tiny log cabin that was built by his grandfather, Rev. William Wise Handy, a minister in the African Methodist Episcopal (AME)

Church. His father, Rev. Charles Bernard Handy, also was a pastor in the AME Church. William Christopher studied the organ at an early age, honoring his father's preference for a traditional music education over the secular choices that the younger Handy had begun to show an interest in early on. By age 15, he again showed a preference for popular music and took off with a traveling minstrel show. This was short-lived, so he returned to Florence. After receiving a degree from the Huntsville Teachers Agricultural and Mechanical College in 1892, Handy formed a quartet and set out on a quest for the St. Louis World Fair, only to find that he had arrived a year early, it had been postponed. What followed was a year of poverty and desperation. He experienced the same blues that he was to hear in the songs and chants of field hands and former slaves. W.C. Handy accepted a position as the conductor of an African American band, the Knights of Pythias, in Clarksdale, MS from 1903 to 1909. While touring, Handy began sampling what he called Negro folk music throughout the Mississippi Delta and the rest of the South. His translation of these field songs and chants to structured, musical compositions brought the blues to a national and international stage.

Three years after moving to Memphis in 1912, Handy befriended a recent graduate and valedictorian of Atlanta University, Harry Herbert Pace, who also was a protégé of W.E.B. Dubois. Together, they founded the Pace and Handy Music company. Both moved to New York City around 1920, just in time to be catapulted into the middle of the Harlem Renaissance. Pace and Handy would part ways with the former creating Black Swan Phonograph Company, America's first African American record label. Handy went on to achieve substantial wealth and acclaim as a composer, author, folklorist, conductor and "Father of the Blues." His compositions include The Memphis Blues, Aunt Hagar's Blues, Beale Street Blues, Chantez-Les-Bas (Sing 'Em Low), St. Louis Blues, and Yellow Dog Blues, to name a few. His compositions have been celebrated and performed by the legends of Jazz: Duke Ellington, Pearl Bailey, Eartha Kit, Louis Armstrong, Cab Callaway, Nat King Cole, Lena Horne and many, many others. Upon his death in 1958, his life was celebrated with a funeral at Harlem's historic Abyssinian Baptist Church. Attendees numbered more than 2,500 while another 150,000 lined Harlem's West 138th street to say goodbye. "A thirty-piece brass band of Handy's fellow Masons, recalling his first musical employment as a bandleader, played their accompaniment to his body's arrival." During the funeral service, Abyssinian's Pastor, the Rev Adam Clayton Powell Jr., delivered a stirring eulogy to Handy: "...Gabriel now has an understudy...And when the last trumpet shall sound, I am sure that W.C. Handy will be there to bury this world, as a sideman...No more the problems of Beale Street. No more the irritations of Memphis. No more the vexation of the St. Louis woman..." (page 229, *W.C. Handy: The Life and Times of the Man who Made the Blues*, David Robertson, Alfred A. Knopf, a Division of Random House, Inc., 2009).

Handy's presence is felt throughout Memphis, but nowhere more so than on Beale Street. A statue of W.C. Handy, with cornet in hand, stands among the trees at the center of Beale Street in W.C. Handy Park.

All that has been said and written about Beale Street justly contributes to its stature as a legendary thoroughfare. The U.S. Congress passed a resolution in 1977 designating this fabled street as the birth place of the blues. While it is well known that jug bands and blues artists gave life to this gathering place, Beale Street was more than the music it nourished. It was the heart of the city's African American community, a place where African American entrepreneurs, professionals, and just plain ordinary folk struggled to survive. Foremost among them was Robert Reed Church Sr. He was born into slavery in Holly Springs, MS in 1839. Upon the death of his mother, Emmeline, in 1851, Church was granted his freedom and went to live with his father, Charles B. Church. He served as his father's apprentice aboard a steamship that sailed between Memphis, TN and New Orleans, LA, rising to the rank of steward. This was an apprenticeship that would later serve the young Church well in life, because he learned the nuances of the hospitality service industry, how to elevate it to an art form. After spending almost a decade with his father, Church moved to Memphis and proceeded to amass a fortune in real estate. Robert R Church Sr. quickly became renowned for his philanthropic heart. After the yellow fever epidemic of 1878, the city of Memphis faced financial peril. Church helped save the city from financial collapse by being the first to purchase a city bond for $1,000. His ventures included the establishment of a hotel, restaurant and saloon. In 1889, Robert Church filled a major void in Memphis life by purchasing six acres of land and building the Church Park and Auditorium on Beale Street, near the intersection of 4th and Turley. It became one of the most celebrated entertainment venues in the South as well as the United States. The auditorium seated more than 2,000 and hosted leaders and speakers that ranged from Booker T. Washington to President Theodore Roosevelt to James Weldon Johnson. As one of the most exquisite stops on the "Chittlin Circuit," Church Park and Auditorium also was celebrated for its house orchestra, led by none other than W.C. Handy, father of the blues. Other legendary performers included Cab Calloway, Mahalia Jackson, Duke Ellington, the Fisk Jubilee Singers and the like. A true renaissance man, Robert Church, Sr. also founded the Solvent Savings Bank & Trust Company in 1908. One of their first loans was provided to the historic Beale Street Baptist Church, thus saving it from foreclosure. The Solvent Savings Bank financing enabled Beale Street Baptist Church to retire their original loan, provided relief from old debtors and gave them more favorable terms in a new loan.

Robert R. Church Sr. also was one of the South's earliest political activists. His establishment of the Church Park and Auditorium was in response to the absence of park, recreation and entertainment options for the African American Community in Memphis at the turn of the Twentieth Century. He also owned real estate investments in Washington DC where one of his tenants was the legendary poet Paul Laurence Dunbar. As a political activist, he counted among his confidants historic figures in African American history such as Frederick Douglas, Booker T. Washington and W.E.B Dubois.

Mary Church Terrell was the daughter of Robert R Church Sr. and his first wife, Louisa Ayers. She graduated from Oberlin College in 1884, becoming one of the 1st African American Women to earn a Bachelor's Degree in the United States. Her accomplishments over 8 decades figured prominently in the history of Women's Suffrage and Civil Rights in America. She was a founding member of the National Association for the Advancement of Colored People. Her younger step brother, Robert R Church Jr, oversaw his father's business and philanthropic interests following Robert R Church Sr.'s death in 1912. He took over management of the Church Park and Auditorium, became President of the Solvent Savings Bank and Trust Company and oversaw the large real estate holdings that his father had acquired. Where Robert R. Church was a legendary entrepreneur in Memphis history, Robert R Church Jr. devoted much of his life to political activism and equal rights for African Americans. The younger Church founded the Lincoln Republican League in 1916, an organization dedicated to registering African American voters, and the Memphis Chapter of the NAACP in 1917.

Ida B. Wells also was born a slave in Holly Springs, MS in 1862. The yellow fever that plagued the region for nearly a decade took her parents' lives in 1876, so she moved to Memphis to help raise her siblings. In 1884, she established her reputation as an advocate of freedom by refusing to give up her seat to a white man on a train owned by the Chesapeake and Ohio Railroad Company. She was forcibly removed. She immediately filed a discrimination law suit against the railroad company, won in lower court, which subsequently was appealed and overturned by the Tennessee Supreme Court. Her challenge won her a regional audience. The pastor of the Beale Street Baptist Church, Rev. R. Nightingale, and Wells successfully launched the Free Speech and Headlight, the first newspaper in the United States owned or co-owned by an African American woman. She eventually left Memphis and moved to Chicago, continuing her crusade as a women's suffragist, anti-lynching advocate and equal rights advocate. She, with Mary Church Terrell, also was one of the founding members of the NAACP, in 1909.

Memphis is rich in American lore and music history. From the historically black college, Lemoyne-Owen University (one of the nation's oldest), to the home of Elvis Presley, to the Civil Rights Museum, there is much to see and much to appreciate in this beautiful city.

JAZZ/BLUES/REGGAE:

B.B. King's Blues Club

Location: 143 Beale Street
Telephone: 901-524-KING
Clientele: Young/Mature Adult
Format: Memphis Music (R&B)/Blues
Calendar: Live Entertainment Nightly
Cover/Minimum: Yes/No
Dress: Classy
URL: www.bbkingclubs.com

Comments: B. B. King's Blues Club is a perfect venue for the blues and R&B oldies. I adopted it as one of my favorite clubs the minute I first walked in the door in 1994: King's is a throwback to times of old, when house parties reigned supreme. That's what you get every evening: patrons throng to the dance floor or engage in high-spirited audience response whenever the band hits an irresistible groove. A number of photos adorn the walls, including one of the "Blue Boys," B. B. King with Elvis Presley, as well as photos of Sam and Dave, Al Green, Muddy Waters, and Johnny Taylor. During the 1990s, the King B's, featuring Ruby Wilson, rocked the house seven nights a week. Rarekas Bonds, one of Ruby's "kids," often would come in and dance for you - he's the boy who tumbled across the screen in the Tom Cruise movie *The Firm*. B. B. King performs about twice each year. Other national acts have included blues stars such as the late Clarence "Gatemouth" Brown, the late Albert Collins, Buddy Guy, and Irma Thomas. Paul McCartney's band, Aerosmith, and Eric Clapton have sat in. B. B. King's also puts on special tributes. One of the most popular was a Stax Records revue that included a tribute to the late great R&B star Otis Redding, and featured his grandson Otis Redding III, Booker T. and the MG's, Sam Moore, the Memphis Horns, and Eddie Floyd. Blind Mississippi Morris currently is one of the featured acts, hailed by many as one this era's newest generation of authentic, Delta Blues men. Blues guitarist, vocalist and octogenarian Carl Darvin Drew also is a must-experience. With over seven decades as a performer and entertainer, he still is doing the blues right. Preston Shannon, out of Olive Branch, MS, is yet another Memphis favorite who often is featured here. B. B. King's main dining room forms a semicircle around the dance floor and stage. An alcove on the second floor also affords comfortable dining while allowing a panoramic view of the stage. The menu ranges from USDA filet mignon to the Southern fried catfish to Cajun carbonara. One of the most requested desserts is the homemade banana bread pudding topped with bourbon glaze and banana caramel sauce. Their corn bread muffins, sweet cole slaw, BBQ beans and collard greens are just the sides to round off a great meal. Although the club seats 400, reservations are recommended. The restaurant serves lunch and dinner daily beginning at 11:00 AM.

JAZZ/BLUES/REGGAE:

Blues City Café

Location: 138 Beale Street
Telephone: 901-526-3637
Clientele: Young/Mature Adult
Format: R&B/Blues/Jazz/Rockabilly.
Calendar: Live Entertainment Nightly
Cover/Minimum: Yes/No
Dress: Casual/Classy
URL: www.bluescitycafe.com

Comments: Blues City Café has been one of the most happening clubs on Beale Street since it opened in March 1991. In fact, it's the place where Beale Street musicians and club employees go for late-night dining and more blues. The club features an attractive dining room on one side and a lounge on the other. The music of choice is blues, of course, and Memphis-flavored R&B. Albert King, Booker T. Laury, Charlie Musselwhite, Rufus Thomas, Clarence "Gatemouth" Brown and Richie Havens are just some of the national touring acts that have performed here. Preston Shannon, a Bullseye Blues recording artist, was the featured act for many years. The Memphis Horns had the release party here for their first solo album, Flame Out. The club's current focus is local Memphis bands. They also feature regional, touring acts at least once per month. Brad Birkedhal & the Burnin' Love Band perform weekly. Also performing weekly—The Masqueraders, an R&B group whose roots date back to the 1950s, will regale you with harmonies that recall the Manhattans, Chilites and Stylistics from the golden era of R&B. The group recorded numerous singles during the '60s and '70s, and two albums, *Everybody Wanna Live On* and *Love Anonymous*, produced by the late, great Isaac Hayes on his Hot Buttered Soul label. Blues City Café features an outstanding menu that includes barbecue ribs, fried catfish, and their most popular entree, the famous oven broiled Memphis strip. Former President Bill Clinton, former U.S. Representative Harold Ford, Sr., actor Samuel L. Jackson, actor Robert DeNiro, and NBA legend Jerry West are among the legion of celebrities who have visited this popular venue. Blues City Café is one Memphis establishment that is carrying on the Beale Street tradition in grand fashion.

JAZZ/BLUES/REGGAE:

Huey's

Location: 77 S. 2nd Street
Telephone: 901-527-2700
Clientele: Young/Mature Adult
Format: Memphis Music (R&B)/Blues/Jazz
Calendar: see website calendar
Cover/Minimum: Yes/No
Dress: Casual/Classy
URL: www.hueyburger.com

Comments: In a city where such offerings are limited, Huey's has provided a jazz venue for more than 18 years. Still, it owes its first allegiance to the blues. The list of blues artists who have either headlined here or sat in with the house band is enormous. "Big Joe" Williams held his last performance here. Matt "Guitar" Murphy, George Thorogood, Son Seals, and Koko Taylor have also put on memorable performances. One of the really special times to catch a show at Huey's is during the week of the annual Blues Music Awards, formerly named the Handy Awards, an event that honors the top blues artists of the past year as well as key individuals celebrated for keeping blues alive in America. The Midtown Jazzmobile had been the featured jazz act at Huey's since the mid-1970s, although the cast of musicians changed somewhat over the years. Jim Spake plays a mean saxophone (baritone, tenor, and soprano) and has been one of the best reasons to catch their act. This group of talented Memphis musicians played everything from bebop to contemporary. Performances start at 4:00 PM; however, get there by 3:30 PM for a good seat. The Memphis Soul Revue is among a current cadre of Memphis talent that rocks the house with covers of the greats from the Stax /Volt era; oldies but goodies as performed by the late Otis Redding, Aretha Franklin and Eddie Floyd. The club undergoes a metamorphosis as the evening goes on and the jazz crowd gives way to the blues crowd. The blues gets underway at 9:00 PM. Again, getting there a half hour early improves your chance of getting a good seat, the closer to the band, the better. While the club normally holds about 120, on some Sundays that number swells to almost 200. Another reason to check Huey's out is their menu of continental cuisine, hamburgers (voted the city's best for nearly 25 years running), and assorted sandwiches. The restaurant opens daily at 11:00 AM for lunch and dinner, serving until around 3:00 AM. Owing to its immense popularity and success, Huey's has expanded to seven locations, featuring four restaurants in Memphis and single venues in Cordova, TN, Collierville, TN and Southaven, MS. Check out their website to see what each venue has to offer during your visit to the Memphis area.

JAZZ/BLUES/REGGAE:

King's Palace Café

Location: 162 Beale Street
Telephone: 901-521-1851
Clientele: Mature Adult
Format: Memphis Music (R&B)/Blues
Calendar: Live Entertainment Nightly (Mar - Sept)
Cover/Minimum: Yes/No
Dress: Classy
URL: www.kingspalacecafe.com

Comments: King's Palace Café, opened in 1989, is a sedate blues and R&B supper club that has gained widespread popularity among older Memphis residents and tourists. The music is toned down, the lights are low, and the atmosphere is rather chic as Beale Street establishments go. While many clubs in the celebrated neighborhood offer the atmosphere of a frolicking dance party, patrons of King's Palace Café are more interested in a venue where they can sit back and relax, feast on a good meal, and enjoy the music. National jazz artists occasionally are featured here, the most memorable act having been Maynard Ferguson in 1991. Guitarist David Bowen captivates the room with Sunday through Thursday with a wide ranging repertoire featuring Blues and Jazz. Michaelyn Oby and The Memphis Jazz Trio are among Memphis' top jazz artists, entertaining King's Palace Café patrons each Friday and Saturday. The first person many visitors are likely to meet when they approach this elegant venue is the "Mayor of Beale Street," also known as the "Ambassador of Beale Street," Rudy Williams, a renowned Memphis trumpeter who has been regaling folks with blues notes and anecdotes for decades. The music generally runs from 7:00 PM to 11:00 PM. Their menu choices range from shrimp & crawfish étouffée to Memphis style barbecue to beef and salmon steaks. Lunch begins daily, Mon – Fri @ 11:00 AM; breakfast is available from 8:00 AM on Saturday and Sunday.

JAZZ/BLUES/REGGAE:

Marmalade Restaurant and Lounge

Location: 153 G. E. Patterson Avenue
Telephone: 901-522-8800
Clientele: Young/Mature Adult
Format: Blues/Jazz/R&B
Calendar: Live Entertainment Fri - Sun
Cover/Minimum: Yes/No
Dress: Casual/Classy

Comments: During the early 1980s, there were few opportunities for African American performers to showcase their talents in Memphis. The Beale Street renovation was still a few years off. But L. B. Smith, a longtime teacher in the Memphis public schools, and his wife Mae, a retiree from the postal system, harbored a dream of owning a restaurant and lounge. After extensive research into the Memphis entertainment market, they opened Marmalade in 1982. The result was an immediate success. The club is an attractive, spacious building adjacent to two Memphis landmarks: the Civil Rights Museum (Lorraine Motel), and the office of the *Tri-State Defender*, the city's only African American-owned newspaper. The Duncan Sisters, Ruby Wilson, and the Smith's son Audi were among the club's first headliners. It also has featured top regional acts such as Joyce Cobb, Willie Covington, Chic and Melinda Rogers. The club has a softly lit dining room, a lounge, a TV room, and a private banquet area. In addition to the fine entertainment, Marmalade offers an outstanding menu of Southern cuisine. The house specialty is seafood gumbo. Many find the grilled pork chops irresistible. De Barge, the late jazz virtuoso Arthur Prysock, and Maurice White (Earth, Wind and Fire) are but a few of the celebrities who have visited. Stop by and enjoy the entertainment, the food, and Mae Smith's gracious Southern hospitality.

JAZZ/BLUES/REGGAE:

Mr. Handy's Blues Hall

Location: 174 Beale Street
Telephone: 901-528-0150
Clientele: Young/Mature Adult
Format: Blues
Calendar: Live Entertainment Varies
Cover/Minimum: Yes/No
Dress: Casual/Classy

Comments: Mr. Handy's Blues Hall is adjacent to Rum Boogie Cafe. In fact, a door donated by the Memphis Blues Society connects them. This door says much about the venue at Blues Hall – it's adorned with covers from program booklets for the annual Handy Awards. The club's design is reminiscent of an authentic old blues honky-tonk. Intimate and small, it's like the mythical smoked-filled room where blues acts of yesteryear performed until the wee hours and the patrons danced the night away.

Guitarist Freddy Harris and company

The walls are accented by old portraits of Beale Street residents, dressed in the high fashions typical there during the early 1930s. Delta blues is the music of choice here. Patrons often spend an evening traversing back and forth between the party at Rum Boogie's and the down-home ambiance of Blues Hall. The Dr. Feelgood Potts Band packs the house from Friday to Sunday. Appreciative patrons either dance to the music or sit in rapt attention as Dr. Feelgood weaves Delta Blues with wit and narrative. One cover gains admission to both.

JAZZ/BLUES/REGGAE:

Rum Boogie Cafe

Location: 182 Beale Street
Telephone: 901-528-0150
Clientele: Young/Mature Adult
Format: Blues/Memphis Music (R&B)
Calendar: Live Entertainment Nightly
Cover/Minimum: Yes/No
Dress: Casual/Classy
URL: www.rumboogie.com

Comments: The Rum Boogie Cafe has been one of the most popular clubs on Beale Street since it opened in 1984. Like many establishments in the neighborhood, the décor is alive with graffiti art and guitars autographed by music legends that have played here including Albert Collins, Bo Didley, Willie Dixon, Billy Gibbons of ZZ Top, and the late Stevie Ray Vaughan. The main room has a stage, a dance floor, and ample seating. A spiral staircase leads to the second-floor alcove where you can dine as well as look down on the stage. The neon sign that hangs above the stage was once the marquis for the Stax Recording Studio. Over 150 guitars hang from the ceilings, signed by music legends such as Kenny Loggins, Pinetop Perkins, Little Milton, Leon Russell, Lou Rawls, and many, many others. Don McMinn and the Rum Boogie Band held court at

Rum Boogie's for more than nine years until 1994, when McMinn left to go on tour and record. The current house band is The Boogie Blues Band, featuring local favorite James Govan. They have been holding court at Rum Boogie for the last 15 years. In addition to the fantastic entertainment that is a staple, Rum Boogie Cafe boasts a menu that includes a seafood gumbo that has been rated tops in the city by the Annual Rajun Cajun Crawfish Festival & Gumbo Cook-off held each April. You also will want to try their red beans & rice, fried catfish and barbecue ribs. The cafe is open for lunch and dinner daily from 11 AM. This is one of Beale Street's feature attractions. Don't miss an opportunity to take in some hot blues and R&B here while visiting Memphis.

DINING:

Alcenia's

Location: 317 Main ST
Telephone: 901-523-0200
Proprietor: Betty Joyce Chester-Tamayo
Dress: Casual/Classy
Menu: Soul Food
Price: Modest
Hours: Tues – Fri 11:00 AM – 5:00 PM; Fri - Sat 9:00 AM – 3:00 PM
URL: www.alcenias.com/

Comments:

Betty Joyce Chester-Tamayo founded her restaurant in 1997. Before that, the Lemoyne-Owens business School graduate worked for Federal Express. In 1996, she suffered the tragic loss of her son in a motorcycle accident. Grief stricken, she vowed to never work for anyone else again. In short, she decided to become an entrepreneur and opened Alcenia's. BJ Chester-Tamayo, inspired by her mother, Alcenia's, cooking. She adopted many of her mother's recipes. In doing so, her restaurant has become a favorite among locals and tourists alike. Be sure to try their fried pork, chicken or catfish served with cabbage, green beans, mac & cheese or candied yams. If you want to take a bit of the Alcenia's experience home with you, ask for the canned preserves & jellies; delicious apricot, pear peach or fig, all sold by the pint.

DINING:

Cozy Corner

Location: 745 North Parkway
Telephone: 901-527-9158
Proprietor: Desiree Robinson & Family
Dress: Casual
Menu: Soul Food
Price: Modest
Hours: Tues - Sat 11:00 AM – 9:00 PM
URL: www.cozycornerbbq.com

Comments: The late Raymond Robinson, Sr., who had made a living building Titan Missiles for Martin Marietta, returned to Memphis in 1966 in search of business opportunities. In 1976, he took the entrepreneurial plunge and achieved enormous success. His Cozy Corner Restaurant has evolved into a family affair that ranks among the city's best. On my first visit in 1991, I immediately felt at home when greeted by hostess Neval Robinson, Raymond Sr.'s mother, who has since passed away. Perhaps she knew that I too was from Louisiana, but more likely, that just was her way. She welcomed you with a warm smile and ensured that you were comfortable, while simultaneously tending to her great-grandchildren who sometimes dropped by to do their homework. Barbecue pork, beef, Cornish hen, and turkey are the specialties. While the ribs are most popular, smoked turkeys are big around the Christmas holidays. In December 1993, patrons walked out carrying smoked turkeys by the armloads - more than 250 on the weekend before Christmas! One of the keys to the delicious flavor of Cozy Corner's ribs is the dry rub, which are sprinkled on after the excess fat trimmed away. The rub, which is made entirely of spices, penetrates the meat by way of its natural juices. Slow-cooking the ribs for two to three hours is the final step. The result is superb. Throwing down some delicious ribs is but one of the pleasures of a meal at Cozy Corner. Raymond Sr. used to regale folks for hours on end with stories about Memphis life and lore. During my first visit in 1991, I was enjoying one of Raymond Sr.'s stories when James Alexander, of Memphis' legendary Bar-Kays, joined us at our booth, participating in an even more engaging conversation. Entertainers and celebrities seem to be drawn to this establishment. Cybil Shepherd stopped by and filmed a scene from her movie *Our Town* right on the premises. A scene from *Coming From Africa* also was filmed here. Bon Appétit, Business Week, Food & Wine, and Gourmet magazines all have featured this landmark establishment. Cozy Corner is one of those places where eating is just half the fun. Southern hospitality and good old-fashioned conversation are the added attractions.

DINING

Four Way Grill

Location: 998 Mississippi Blvd
Telephone: 901-507-1519
Proprietor: Willie Earl Bates
Dress: Casual
Menu: Soul Food
Price: Very Modest
Hours: Tues – Sat, 11:00 AM – 7:00 PM; Sun, 11:00 AM – 5:00 PM

Comments: The Four Way Grill is one of Memphis's most-celebrated soul-food restaurants, widely chronicled in official tour guides and in a number of books about the city's history and cuisine. It is also one of those landmarks institutions that have managed to survive more than half a century. Irene Cleaves and her late husband, Clint, founded the restaurant in 1946. The original restaurant was sparse on décor, but heavy on tradition, enjoying a long list of customers whose allegiance spanned generations. The list of visitors during the 1950s thru 1990s included the Reverend Dr. Martin Luther King, Jr., the Reverend Jesse Jackson, Nat King Cole, Alex Haley, "Sugar Ray" Robinson, Gladys Knight and the Pips, and Lionel Hampton. On my first visit, I couldn't help but think, "if these walls could talk, what a story they could tell!" The booths and tables were worn, but what was prepared and delivered when you ordered was just as the citizens of Memphis proudly proclaimed: traditional soul food prepared in down-home fashion, and plenty of it! I enjoyed a feast of Southern fried chicken, turnip greens, and northern beans. Other popular items from the menu included chitterlings, baked beef spare ribs, ham hocks, and fried catfish. The stewed apples and yam patties were fantastic. When you entered the Four Way Grill up until the late 1990s, you got both an incredible meal and a big slice of American history.

Upon the passing of Irene Cleaves, the doors of the Four Way Grill closed. It lay dormant for several years. Rumors of condemnation for this historic property prevailed, the public notice finally confirming its eminent demise between 1999 and 2000. Retired insurance salesman Willie Earl Bates heard the news and was alarmed. He had assembled newspapers for his delivery route on these very doorsteps when he was a boy. Bates came out of retirement, took immediate action and rescued Four Way Grill. He secured financing for the purchase, not only of the restaurant, but two adjacent buildings. His restoration and expansion of the original Four Way Grill is a work or art. With the help of some faithful cooks from the late Irene Cleaves' former staff, the food is as delicious as it has ever been and Memphians are ecstatic. Another generation of celebrities continues to grace the doors of this storied establishment. The children of the late Rev. Dr. Martin Luther King Jr. ate here as a family while visiting Memphis: the late Yolonda King, Martin Luther King III, Dexter Scott King and Bernice King. Other noted guests have included the late Memphis legend Isaac Hayes, Rev. Al Sharpton, former New Orleans Mayor Clarence Ray Nagin, Jr., and actress Melba Moore. On a recent visit in July, 2010, I had a delicious meal of southern fried catfish, corn and lima beans. The Four Way Grill continues to be a "must experience" when visiting Memphis.

Restaurant owner Willie Bates samples the goods.

Four Way Grill boasts a new, modern makeover.

DINING:

Jim Neely's Interstate Bar-B-Que

Location: 2265 South 3rd Street
Telephone: 901-775-2304
Proprietor: Jim Neely
Dress: Casual/Classy
Menu: Barbecue
Price: Modest
Hours: Mon – Thurs 11:00 AM – 11:00 PM; Fri – Sat 11:00 AM – 2:00 AM; Sun 12:00 PM – 10:00 PM
URL: www.interstatebarbecue.com

Comments: While traveling throughout the South on insurance business during the late 1970s, barbecue lover Jim Neely began to think about devoting more time to entrepreneurial pursuits. He decided to convert a recently acquired building into a barbecue restaurant and launched his new business in March 1980. It was an immediate and resounding success. Neely takes great satisfaction in putting out a quality product. One of the key elements to his barbecue's popularity is the pit. It's Jim Neely's own design, and there are only six in existence. (Jim has two, and his two nephews of Neely's Barbecue have two each.) I won't reveal the design of these pits, but I will say that the fire is offset from the meat. Other key elements include the use of a select cut of brisket (away from the fat or muscle) and ribs that are exclusively "three and down." Jim Neely only uses corn-fed, Midwestern hogs.

The slow-cooking process, ranging from three and a half hours for ribs to fifteen hours for pork brisket, locks in the flavor that is uniquely Jim Neely's. He prepares 60 quarts of sauce, four times daily. His sauce, with a tomato base of 33 ½ percent solids, features a special blend of herbs and spices. Jim Neely's Interstate BAR-B-Que is very much a family affair. His wife, Barbara, has been at his side from the very beginning, working long hours and loving every minute of it. His oldest son, Kelvin, manages the evening shift. Another son, Keith, manages their second restaurant at 150 W. Stateline Rd in South Haven, MS. Kelvin Jr., and a recent Memphis State University graduate, oversees the restaurant's USDA certified warehouse which contains two more ovens and houses a bustling packing and shipping operation. They ship their delicious barbecue and sauces by FedEx Overnight throughout the country. Jim Neely and his family also own two restaurants at the Memphis International Airport (Terminal B: Concourse B Rotunda and B14) and are part owners of the airport's Blue Note Café (Passenger Connector B-A). You either can stop in for delicious barbecue ribs, brisket, shoulders and chicken or order online. Patrons are attracted to Jim Neely's Interstate Bar-B-Que from all corners of Memphis society and from all parts of the country. Over the years, Neely's has received an avalanche of favorable publicity. *People* Magazine, for example, published the results of a national survey in 1989 rating Neely's second in the country behind the legendary Arthur Bryant's Rib House of Kansas City, Missouri. Vogue Magazine has cited them as the best commercial barbecue in Memphis. George Carlin, Susan Sarandon, and the late Memphis icon Rufus Thomas are among the legions of celebrities who have dropped in for Neely's special fare. This restaurant should definitely be included among your top dining choices when visiting the city.

DINING:

Lunchbox Eats
Location: 288 S. Fourth ST
Telephone: 901-526-0820
Proprietor: Chef Kaia Brewer
Dress: Casual/Classy
Menu: Soulful Fusion, Gourmet Sandwiches
Price: Modest-Moderate
Hours:
URL: www.lunchboxeats.com

Comments: Lunchbox Eats is a self-described Gourmet, Eclectic & Soulful Sandwich Shop in Downtown Memphis. The restaurant was founded in 2010 by Chef Kaia Brewer after attending Johnson & Wales and serving a brief stint as executive chef at the Memphis' downtown Doubletree Hotel. Everything about the place is school themed, from décor to menu items to the mural of the school bus as you drive up to the building. Her tribute to all things school is the result of being raised by parents who both were long time teachers in the Memphis Public School system.

Highlights from the menu include:

Homeroom Chicken & Grids

"Our version of Chicken & Waffles is Deep Fried Chicken sandwiched between Two Golden Brown Cheddar Waffles, topped with Muenster Cheese served with Whole Grain Honey Mustard or Green Tomato Relish"

Graduation Burger
"Nestled between Toasted White Bread a Juicy Cut of an American Classic, MEATLOAF- tunneled with Pepperjack cheese, crowned with Creamy Mashed Potatoes,
Tomato Gravy and Crispy Tabasco Onions'

3rd Period Smoking Birds
"Slow smoked Black Cherry Wood pulled Cajun Turkey, Molasses Chicken Succulent Duck and Veggie Slaw are stacked on Fresh Baked Wheat Bread served with Tri-Bird Pan Liquor, choice of BBQ Sauce or Green Tomato Relish"

On my 1st visit, I tried their "Principals' Office Link," an awesome dish featuring fried eggs, lettuce, and tomatoes atop a smoked hot link and nestled in a spicy grilled sauce. Lunchbox Eats is a favorite stop for employees of the surrounding business district, public service workers and students alike. The restaurant is located just southeast of the FEDEX Forum, on the corner of Fourth and Linden Avenue. This is an exciting, eclectic eatery that is a must experience while visiting Memphis.

DINING:

Sweetie Pie's
Location: 349 Beale ST
Telephone: TBD
Proprietor: Chef Robbie Montgomery
Dress: Casual/Classy
Menu: Soul Food
Price: TBD
Hours: TBD
URL: www.sweetiepieskitchen.com

Comments: Much of Memphis excitedly awaits "Miss Robbies" newest restaurant venture. The former backup singer with legendary icons Ike & Tina Turner, the Rolling Stones and Dr. John, to put it mildly, has come a long way. Born in nearby Columbus, Mississippi, she and her family relocated to St. Louis at the end of World War II. Like many African Americans in the Post War South, they migrated north, seeking better opportunities for a growing family that were not so readily available in rural Mississippi. Robbie Montgomery's musical journey began in St. Louis' Temple Baptist Church where she sang in the gospel choir. She left home in the early 1960's and toured with Ike & Tina as a member of the Ikettes. After a musical career that spanned four decades, from the early 1950's to the late 1980s, a collapsed lung forced Miss Robbie to stop singing professionally. She then undertook a 10 year career in health care where she cared for a long time patient, who, as fate would have it, became a lifelong friend and benefactor. The patient was the late St. Louis developer and redevelopment guru, Leon Straus. He and his wife Mary provided crucial funding that helped Robbie launch Sweetie Pie's Soul Food Restaurant. She and her son, Tim Norman, opened two more Sweetie Pie's in St. Louis and established a tradition that St. Louis has embraced as its very own, the city's most important soul food venues.

Several months before launching their "Upper Crust" restaurant, Robbie's son Tim was tossing around the idea of a TV show based on the family and their interaction while running their soul food restaurants. He pitched the concept to a local St. Louis media company, Coolfire Media, sometimes in April, 2011. Coolfire loved the idea, took it to the staff at Oprah Winfrey Network (OWN) and Oprah reportedly embraced it immediately. OWN had just launched in January, but was experiencing limited success. "Welcome to Sweetie Pie's" debuted in October, 2011 and quickly experienced widespread acclaim. Miss Robbie, Tim Norman and his fiancé Jenae join a cast of family members and employees whose struggles and triumphs in running the family restaurants have become "must experience" viewing for an American public, especially among African American Women. A ravenous public continues to tune in for "seconds" and more. "Welcome to Sweetie Pies" is serving up heaping helpings to one million viewers per episode. Needless to say, Robbie Montgomery St. Louis Restaurants are experiencing lines out the door. Hungry guests pour out of tour busses in order to take in the ambiance and savor some "down home cooking." Miss Robbie and family have created a brand that has gone viral.

Memphis can't wait to roll out the red carpet and extend a hearty "Welcome to Sweetie Pie's." Beale Street was an important stop on the "Chittlin Circuit" as early as the "turn of the 20th Century. Miss Robbie and the Ike & Tine Turner Revue played this street during the 1960s, even staying at the legendary Lorene Motel across town. Ironically, her Memphis Sweetie Pie's is located less than a block from the former "Church Park & Auditorium," a landmark venue seating over 2000. The legendary Robert Church, SR. built this establishment in 1899. None other than the "Father of the Blues," W.C. Handy, was his house bandleader. Even before Washington DC's Howard Theatre and New York's Appolo Theatre, this incredible concert and banquet hall was hosting historic figures such as President Theodore Wilson, Booker T. Washington and James Weldon Johnson; jazz legends Duke Ellington, Louis Armstrong, and Cab Calloway also held court here. Given the national brand of Sweetie Pie's, Miss Robbie's Memphis digs also has the potential of providing an enormous economic and cultural boost to the Memphis landscape. Record Producer and Music Executive Matthew Knowles (Beyoncé's father) has been rumored to be a potential partner. If this partnership comes to fruition, the economic impact could be even greater. While the legacy of the Robert R. Church family and their impact on Memphis and American history is profound, Robbie Montgomery's "Sweetie Pie's" could help fill the void of an African American presence that has long been absent from Beale Street.

Update: As of 23 Dec, 2015, the status of Sweetie Pie's move to Memphis is on hold. Local fans of the hit TV show and foodies throughout Memphis still are poised to extend a hearty "welcome to Sweetie Pie's." follow ongoing developments at "Tennessee's breaking news leader," www.commercialappeal.com or Sweetie Pie's website at, www.sweetiepieskitchen.com.

DINING:

The Bar-B-Que Shop

Location: 1782 Madison Avenue
Telephone: 901-272-1277
Proprietor: Frank Vernon
Dress: Casual/Classy
Menu: Barbecue
Price: Modest
Hours: Mon – Thurs 11:00 AM – 10:00 PM; Fri - Sat 11:00 AM – 11:00 PM
URL: www.dancingpigs.com

Comments: Frank Vernon worked at UPS for 13 years and often would stop by Brady & Lil's for some of their famous barbecue and swap tales with the owner, Brady P. Vinson. During one of those visits, Vinson indicated that he was considering retiring and wanted to know whether Vernon was serious about getting into the business. After some soul searching and deliberation with his wife Hazel, Vernon accepted the opportunity. They negotiated a purchase price and, more importantly, Vinson offered to stay on to show Vernon the ropes, sharing his recipes and other important barbecue secrets. Vernon took this fateful step in 1978. In 1987, he changed the name of the place to The Bar-B-Que Shop to establish more firmly his own identity in the community. He has more than carried on the tradition of this family restaurant, elevating it to even greater heights. He credits his wife and the late Brady's vision as being the keys to his success. Vernon's son Eric often came in to help in the kitchen between his studies at Memphis State University. Frank Vernon says that his method of barbecuing is unique. Vernon slow-cooks his meat over charcoal with oak and hickory logs, placing a foil over the ribs and Boston butt shoulders to retain their juices. His sauces were so good that he sold them to customers by the quart. In 1995, he originated his "Dancing Pigs" marketing campaign in order to capture a mass market. The original barbecue sauce, an all-purpose gourmet sauce and his dry seasoning are sold on the shelves of Kroger grocery stores in Tennessee, Arkansas, Mississippi, Missouri, and Kentucky. His award-winning sauces and meticulous attention to slow cooking the meat result in some of the most incredible ribs you will ever have. The local *Memphis Commercial Appeal,* the *New York Times*, Southern Living, Bon Appetit and *People* magazines heartily agree. Vernon provides catering services to many businesses in the city, including Federal Express, Holiday Inn, and Hewlett-Packard. B. B. King, Cybil Shepherd, and Bobby "Blue" Bland are but a few of the celebrities who have stopped in to sample their delicious ribs.

Brownlee Hall at the historic Lemoyne-Owen University

The Stax Museum of American Soul Music

Traditional Blues at W.C. Handy Park

Bullseye Blues recording artist Preston Shannon
takes in a show at B.B. King's Blues Club

A tribute marker to the late R&B and Memphis music pioneer Rufus Thomas at W.C. Handy Park Historical markers by the Tennessee Historical Commission

4E 83
PEE WEE SALOON
(P. WEE SALOON)
Pee Wee's Saloon was the favorite meeting spot for Memphis musicians in the early 20th Century W. C. Handy used the cigar counter to write out copies of the Beale Street blues for his band members. One of those songs, written for the 1909 political campaign was first named "Mr. Crump," for the Memphis mayor and political boss. Later with new lyrics it became famous as "The Memphis Blues."

4E 119
RUFUS THOMAS, JR.
(Continued from other side)
He had the first hit records for both the Sun and Stax labels. As a popular personality on WDIA, he was the first disc jockey to play Elvis Presley records on a Black radio station. He was the creator of two of the biggest dance crazes of the 1960s--"The Dog" and "The Funky Chicken."

4E 85
IDA B. WELLS
1862-1931
Ida B. Wells crusaded against lynchings in Memphis and the South. In 1892 while editor of the Memphis Free Speech, located in this vicinity, she wrote of the lynching of three Black businessmen. As a result, her newspaper office was destroyed and her life threatened.
(Continued on other side)

4E 85
IDA B. WELLS
1862-1931
(Continued from other side)
After moving to New York, she began an international speaking tour where she influenced the establishment of the British Anti-Lynching Society. She co-founded the NAACP in America and organized the first Black women's political organization. A Chicago housing project is named in her honor.
TENNESSEE HISTORICAL COMMISSION

The Delta Blues Museum, just a short 2 hour
drive down Hwy 61 from Memphis, TN to Clarksdale, MS

NEW ORLEANS, LOUISIANA

New Orleans embodies the spirit of the South. Although the language is obviously English, the flavor is African, French and Spanish. New Orleans' essence is appropriately manifested in its rich jazz heritage. Even before blues and ragtime were being forged in the Mississippi Delta and Missouri Valley in the late 1800s, African Americans in the Crescent City were creating a new music as early as 1730. Enriched by a merger of French, Spanish, and African rhythms, the city also gave birth to Creole and Cajun Cuisines. Creole Cuisine can be described as the convergence of immigrant French and Spanish tastes with those of the indigenous Native American population, African American and Afro-Caribbean. European tastes for beef, pork, wild game, and grains, Native Americans for shrimp, oysters, maize, beans and dried, ground sassafras leaves and Africans with an additional knowledge of rice, okra, and spices were the ingredients with which early New Orleans kitchens perfected their culinary skills in the mid to late 1700s. The art that was produced from these cornerstone ingredients matured into the Creole Cuisine that is loved and sought after today. Cajun Cuisine evolved as more of a marriage of French-Canadian (Acadians), Indian and African cultures, all converging in a delectable collage, emerging as a novel and artistic approach to cooking wild game such as alligator, rabbit and duck, to name a few, accented with rice and covered with thick gravy.

According to many historians, New Orleans is the city that gave birth to America's unique musical art form, jazz, in the late 1800s; however, these musical roots run even deeper. African Slaves were exposed to French compositions and instruments from the moment that French Settlers and Slaves were imported to New Orleans in large number, shortly after Sieur de Bienville founded the City in 1719. French balls and cabarets quickly emerged as their most coveted pastime. Musicians were recruited from the ranks of European immigrants, Free People of Color and African Slaves. Moreover, African Slaves from the region of Senegambia in West Africa imported musical traditions accumulated over the centuries, playing all manner of percussion instruments (Including drums), wind instruments, and stringed instruments such as Koras (similar to banjos). These same slaves also were skilled Artisans (carpenters, metal workers et al), farmers, hunters and fishermen.

In the mid-1700s, slaves were given the opportunity to gather in Congo Square (located within Louis Armstrong Park) every Sunday. Nowhere in America were hundreds of slaves allowed to congregate, play drums and dance freely. Imagine a typical Sunday afternoon where throngs of slaves gathered by tribe, playing the music of their homeland, dancing to native instruments and rhythms. Food cooked in accordance with their African traditions was almost certainly consumed; one pot dishes of West African influence such as *Supa-Kanja* (Oyster Stew) and *Jollof Rice* [(or *Benachin)*, chicken or fish with rice, tomatoes, peppers and spices…]. The opportunities for collaboration, assimilation and growth must have been profound.

Another unique development in the annals of slavery occurred after Louisiana passed into the hands of the Spanish in 1762; African Slaves in New Orleans were given the right to own money and property, to buy their freedom and the right of inheritance. Unlike slaves in the rest of the country, they had tangible evidence that freedom not only was possible, but there was a clear path. Although the Spanish law was repealed after the Louisiana Purchase of 1803, African slaves in New Orleans had experienced unprecedented opportunities for over four decades. This glimpse of freedom was not to be fully realized until the Emancipation Proclamation, more than half a century in the future. Meanwhile, New Orleans then became the largest slave trading port in the United States.

A second wave of French immigrants numbering over 10,000 came to New Orleans from Saint Dominque (now Haiti) after fleeing the *Haitian Revolution* by way of Eastern Cuba in the early 1800s. Two thirds of their numbers were either Free Persons of Color or Slaves. The city of New Orleans once again had a major infusion of Creoles, Creoles of Color and African Slaves. Historian Nicholas Sublette wrote in his *The World That Made New Orleans*, " …All three of the groups that came in 1809-10—white, mulatto and black—had spending six years in Cuba in common, the youngest of them had been born there. Within the city, it's safe to say that no aspect of New Orleans culture remained untouched by their influence." The population of the city had increased two-fold. These events, dating back to the birth of New Orleans, provide a clear picture of what makes The Crescent City different from any other city in America. They also help paint a picture of the emerging forces that percolated in New Orleans, serving as an incubator for a new music and a unique culture.

The list of pioneers among Jazz Musicians in New Orleans is long and storied. Cornetist Buddy Bolden had emerged as the leading practitioner of the new blues and ragtime movement in the late 1890s. He is recalled by early jazz pioneers as the first musician to play blues in a syncopated style. His improvisations on cornet became a signature of the new jazz idiom. After forming his band in 1895, Bolden became the toast of New Orleans. Brass bands had begun to spring up all over the city. By the turn of the century, these bands, most notably Buddy Bolden's, had developed music where the beat was unique in its syncopation and the musicians free to improvise collectively. Native son Louis "Satchmo" Armstrong was pivotal in taking this art form to lofty heights as the United States' musical ambassador from the early 1930s to 1971, the last year of his life. Jazz pioneers from Joe "King" Oliver in the 1920s to Satchmo in the 1930s to current trumpet legend Wynton Marsalis all point to Buddy Bolden as the source, the one to whom they and the world owe a great debt as one of the founders of Jazz.

The list of famous New Orleans musicians continues with giants of jazz such as Sydney Bechet, Jelly Roll Morton, and Edward "Kid" Ory. In blues, there is Antoine "Fats" Domino and departed stars such as Lizzie Douglas aka Memphis Minnie, longtime residents "Professor" Longhair, Clarence "Gatemouth" Brown and nearby Lafayette, Louisiana native Clifton Chenier, to name a few. The city's musical roots within families also run deep. Trombonist Lucien Barbarin traces his lineage back to five generations of musical Barbarins such as his great uncle Isidore Barbarin, a leader of one of the city's early brass bands.

Mahalia Jackson was born in 1911. Her family resided in what many refer to as the Black Pearl section of the Carrollton Neighborhood of New Orleans. Recognized as a music virtuoso as a child, she honed her gospel skills as a member of the youth choir at the Mount Moriah Baptist Church. After moving with her family to Chicago in 1927, her signature contralto voice became widely heralded as a member of the Greater Salem Baptist Church Choir. Her collaborations with gospel pioneer song writers / composers Doris Akers, Rev. William Herbert Brewster and Thomas Dorsey led to numerous gospel hits; "Precious Lord, Take My Hand," "Lord, Don't Move the Mountain," "Move On Up a Little Higher," and "God Is So Good to Me." Mahalia achieved national and international acclaim, becoming universally known as "The Queen of Gospel Music." Her accomplishments were numerous, but none more so than singing at the inauguration of President John F. Kennedy, singing at the historic "March on Washington of 1963 and singing "Precious Lord, Take My Hand" at the funeral of Rev. Dr. Martin Luther King, Jr. With her passing in 1972, the two cities of Chicago and New Orleans were heartbroken, each honoring Mahalia Jackson with the equivalent of state funerals.

Among contemporary New Orleans legends, Ellis Marsalis leads a musical family that includes sons Branford, Delfeayo, Jason, and Wynton; their influence is felt worldwide. The Marsalis Family was recognized as National Endowment of the Arts (NEA) Jazz Masters in 2011, becoming the first family so honored. Aaron Neville and his talented siblings also illuminate the musical landscape of the Crescent City. The late clarinetist Alvin Batiste was yet another among the city's constellation of stars. A renowned educator, composer, author and performer, he founded and taught music at the Jazz Institute at Southern University. He and Ellis Marsalis helped lead the way in fostering education among area youth, providing invaluable platforms for the emergence of a new generation of jazz musicians.

While thousands annually flock to New Orleans' world-famous Mardi Gras celebration and the Jazz & Heritage Festival, the Crescent City also offers many other attractions that make a visit there memorable any time of the year.

JAZZ/BLUES/REGGAE:

Blue Nile

Location: 532 Frenchman Street
Telephone: 504-948-2583
Clientele: Young/Mature Adult
Format: Blues/Jazz/Reggae/Latin
Calendar: Live Entertainment Nightly
Cover/Minimum: Yes/No
Dress: Casual/Classy
URL: www.bluenilelive.com

COMMENTS: The club occupies a building that was built in 1832. It has previously housed The Dream Palace (circa 1970s) and opened as the Blue Nile in 2000. The current management took over operations in 2003. This two -level venue offers a wide range of music options, from hip hop to Afro-Cuban to jazz. The décor is colorful and vibrant. The far wall is adorned with art that General Manager Jessie Paige describes as "Katrina Art." Just before Katrina hit, they boarded up the front of the club with plywood. Upon returning to the Blue Nile as soon as residents were allowed back in the city, his heart was lightened at the discovery of this painting by an unknown artist that covered the entire section of plywood. The storm damage was extensive, but Paige was determined to recover. Troy "Trombone Shorty" Andrews performed at their "grand re-opening." Guests who come here will find that Jessie Paige successfully delivers on his entertainment credo: "Experience the music in four dimensions; dance, sight, hearing and experience." Kermit Ruffins and the Barbecue Swingers hold court on most Friday nights. On any given night you also may catch such New Orleans stars as Grammy Award winner and trumpet virtuoso Irvin Mayfield, Cyril Neville (of the Neville Brothers), "Trombone Shorty" and saxophonist Khris Royal.

Kermit draws a capacity crowd on Friday nights. Patrons begin cuing up around 9:00 PM, but don't expect Ruffin and the Barbecue Swingers until 11:00 PM or so. It's a wait that builds with anticipation as the band begins to saunter inside. The evening explodes from the first note played by showman and trumpet virtuoso Kermit and his hot Barbecue Swingers.

JAZZ/BLUES/REGGAE:

Bullet's Sports Bar

Location: 2441 A P Tureaud Avenue
Telephone: (504) 948-4003
Clientele: Young/Mature Adult
Format: Blues/Jazz/R&B
Calendar: Live Entertainment Tues and Sun
Cover/Minimum: No/No
Dress: Casual/Classy

COMMENTS:

As observed in the introduction to this book, many soul food restaurants historically have been anchors of their respective communities. In the case of Bullets Sports Bar, they have not only been anchors, but in the very literal sense, "a lifeboat." After hurricane Katrina unleashed its fury on the city in 2005, Bullets' owner Rollin "Big Bullet" Garcia Sr. ferried his boat through the flood ravaged streets and rescued many of his neighbors. He took in elderly residents, housing them and feeding them in his apartment above this neighborhood bar. Needless to say, those acts of generosity and kindness further endeared him and *Bullets's* to all of the residents of this 7th Ward Community. Rollin "Little Bullet" Garcia Jr. also helped his father minister to the needs of the community in the aftermath of the storm, hosting cookouts, feeding neighborhood residents and relief workers, letting all know that Bullets' was back in business and there to help revive the community. The younger "Bullet" has taken over the day to day operations and management of the bar.

Bullet's Sports Bar has long been one of New Orleans' best kept secrets. Locals know where it is, when it's open, and of course, "who dat say they gonna beat them Saints?" It is very much a neighborhood bar. Bullets' is sited in a duplex, a long rectangular room with tables lined against the far wall, a few tables in the middle and a very long bar as you enter on the right. Three monitors are the center of attention from the first noon "kickoff" for college and Saints football "in season." Local patrons wax philosophic on everything from President Obama to New Orleans rebuilding to Saint Augustine High School football. On Tuesday afternoons, or maybe early in the evening, the neighborhood right around Bullet's undergoes a transformation. That's when Kermit Washington pulls up in his truck, maybe towing his full barbecue rig. A handful of knowledgeable locals also arrive, setting up barbecue pits all around the block and across the street. The aroma of delicious barbecue permeates the air. Sometime later in the evening, maybe around 7 PM or whenever the spirit moves, Kermit and his Barbecue Swingers take the stage and the party begins. You want to get there well before then because the room begins to fill quickly by 6 PM. Local bands perform most Sunday evenings. This is a local watering hole that's not so secret anymore, thanks to the spotlight of the hugely popular HBO series, Tremé.

JAZZ/BLUES/REGGAE:

Donna's Bar & Grill

Location: 800 N. Rampart Street
Telephone: 504-596-6914
Clientele: Young/Mature Adult
Format: Brass Band Jazz/Traditional/ Straight Ahead/ Blues
Calendar: Live Entertainment Varies
Cover/Minimum: Yes/No
Dress: Casual/Classy
URL: www.donnasbarandgrill.com

Comments: Donna's is located across the street from the entrance to Louis Armstrong Park. It is a modest outpost on the edge of the French Quarter that serves up brass band jazz and down home cooking. On any given night, you might catch a performance by the Tremé Brass Band, or the Leroy Jones Jazz Quartet, or Steve Walker and Friends playing straight ahead to bebop. If you are really lucky, your visit might coincide with an impromptu stop by a brass band parade. Restaurant owner Donna Sims should have an honorary membership on the New Orleans Tourist Bureau. She is all New Orleans jazz all the time. Read "Donna Sez" on her website and you will understand why. Stop by for some great music and a heaping helping of barbecue, Creole, or Soul Cuisine. Charlie Sims cooks up some of the tastiest ribs this side of Memphis. In fact, make this one of your first stops when visiting New Orleans because you most assuredly will want to come back for seconds.

JAZZ/BLUES/REGGAE:

House of Blues

Location: 225 Decatur Street
Telephone: 504-310-4999
Clientele: Young/Mature Adult
Format: Blues/Jazz/R&B/Zydeco
Calendar: Live Entertainment Nightly
Cover/Minimum: Yes/No
Dress: Casual/Classy
URL: www.houseofblues.com

Comments: The grand opening of the House of Blues in January 1994 was one of New Orleans' most anticipated events in many years. Dan Aykroyd and the blues Brothers' Band reunited just to give the club a proper send-off, and blues stalwarts Steve Cropper, Honeyboy Edwards, Robert Jr. Lockwood, Joe Walsh, Junior Wells, and bandleader Paul Shaffer of The David Letterman Show helped round out an all-star cast. The House of Blues has as its mission to showcase the blues in a beautiful setting and to promote harmony among people. They got off to a great start – this is a place where the entire city comes together. If you look at the line-up of blues talent this club offers, it's small wonder why. In May 1994, the calendar featured Bobby "Blue" Bland, Charles Brown, Booker T.

and the MG's, James Cotton, Five Blind Boys from Alabama, Buddy Guy, Queen Latifah, Los Lobos, Taj Mahal, Little Milton, Charlie Musselwhite, John Hammond, the Nighthawks, Otis Rush, Walter "Wolfman" Washington, and the Edgar Winter Band featuring Carmine Appice, to name a few! The stage is the centerpiece of this showcase lounge. Icons of Christian, Jewish, Islamic, Buddhist, and Hindu faiths are painted above it, and every seat, both in the balcony and on the lower level, provides an intimate view. The dining room is an attraction in itself. Recorded blues and live

performances from the blues room are piped softly over the speaker system. The décor is highlighted by handcrafted reliefs of 108 great blues artists on the ceiling. The cuisine is New Orleans style: Creole, regional and international, all served up by award-winning chef Sam McCord. The restaurant is open from 11:30 AM until closing, Wednesday through Sunday. Call first on Mondays and Tuesdays. Their Sunday Gospel brunch runs until 2:00p.m. Reservations are strongly encouraged, especially for the live shows. Don't leave New Orleans without experiencing the House of Blues!

JAZZ/BLUES/REGGAE:

Irvin Mayfield's Jazz Playhouse
at the Royal Sonesta Hotel

Location: 300 Bourbon Street
Telephone: 504-553-2299
Clientele: Young/Mature Adult
Format: Jazz
Calendar: Live Entertainment Nightly
Cover/Minimum: No/No
Dress: Casual/Classy
URL: irvinmayfield.com

Comments: Internationally acclaimed trumpeter Irving M. Mayfield, Jr. has emerged as a genuine New Orleans treasure at the tender age of 31. His many accomplishments are broad and distinguished. Here's a few:

- Nominated by President Barak Obama to the National Council on the Arts, receiving Senate Confirmation on February 11, 2010
- Founded the Institute of Jazz Culture in 2003, serving as Artist-in-Residence at Dillard University from 1995-2005.

- "Appointed the Cultural Ambassador of the City of New Orleans in 2003 by the United States Senate, Congress and other governmental agencies…" (www.basinstreetrecords.com)
- Mayfield, drummer Jason Marsalis and percussionist Bill Summers co-founded Los Hombres Calientes, a Grammy Award-nominated Latin jazz band, in 1998.
- Founded the New Orleans Jazz Orchestra (NOJO), whose goal is to celebrate the rich cultural history of New Orleans jazz and to shape its future growth. Recipient of the 2010 Grammy Award for *Best Large Jazz Ensemble* for its CD Book One on the World Village/Harmonia Mundi label. Partnered with the University of New Orleans and Tulane University.
- The University of New Orleans created the position of Professor of Professional Practice and Artistic Director of the New Orleans Jazz Institute specifically for the versatile Mayfield.

Add to the list above, visionary entrepreneur. In partnership with the Royal Sonesta Hotel, Mayfield leads a bold and creative business model that showcases New Orleans' rich jazz history in a beautiful, romantic setting.

His IM Jazz Playhouse provides entertainment nightly, ranging from sensational jazz, his own band prominently featured, to the risqué Storyville-inspired cabarets of old to scintillating brass bands. During my first visit, I enjoyed a performance by Bob French and the Original Tuxedo Brass Band. The lineage of this band goes all the way back to its founder in 1910, the legendary Oscar "Papa" Celestin, one of the fathers of New Orleans jazz. Upon the death of Papa Celestin in 1954, leadership of the band was passed to trombonist Eddie Pierson for four years, then featured banjoist Albert "Papa" French from 1958 to 1977. Upon the death of his father, the leadership of the band passed into the very capable hands of drummer Bob French. Needless to say, IM's Jazz Playhouse pays tribute to New Orleans jazz history in a way that will both entertain and inspire. Don't miss an opportunity to kick back, relax and experience the tradition of New Orleans jazz in a luxurious, intimate setting.

JAZZ/BLUES/REGGAE:

Maison Bourbon Jazz Club

Location: 641 Bourbon Street
Telephone: 504-522-8818
Clientele: Young/Mature Adult
Format: Jazz
Calendar: Live Entertainment Nightly
Cover/Minimum: No/Yes (1 drink per set)
Dress: Casual/Classy

Comments: Maison Bourbon is a cozy club like many that have appeared on Bourbon Street over the years. The music can run from touristy to scintillating. New Orleans jazz legends that have been regularly featured here include the late trumpeters Thomas Jefferson and Wallace Davenport. Both born during the early 1920s, each left a legacy of excellence on trumpet and in jazz. Their tradition of excellence is carried on today by the incomparable Jamil Sharif, trumpeter, composer and educator, as well as trumpeter extraordinaire, Dwayne Burns.

Trumpeter Dwayne Burns with Michael Torregano on piano, Robert Celerier on trumpet, Rick Bogarton on clarinet, Mark Dwayne on upright, and Hurly Blanchard on drums.

If your timing is right, either masters Sharif or Burns will capture the house during your visit to Maison Bourbon.

JAZZ/BLUES/REGGAE:

Margaritaville

Location: 1104 Decatur Street
Telephone: 504-592-2565
Clientele: Young/Mature Adult
Format: R&B/Cajun/Zydeco
Calendar: Live Entertainment Tues – Sat
Cover/Minimum: Yes/No
Dress: Casual/Classy
URL: www.margaritavilleneworleans.com

Comments: Margaritaville, since its founding in 1993, has emerged as one of the city's most important venues for showcasing the unique rhythms and blues of New Orleans musicians. The building has not always been so – its dubious past includes serving as a slave auction house in the early 1800s and later, as a brothel for children. In more recent times, it housed the Storyville nightclub, also a showcase for New Orleans music, but still rather stark and bare. Singer and author Jimmy Buffet and Sunshine Smith took over the property in 1993 and redeemed it as Margaritaville. The building is now awash in a sea of tropical colors and hues. Replicas of parrots and fish are either suspended from the ceiling or nestled along the walls. As you enter, a grand piano sits on the left, and a small bar is situated at the rear. A low wall divides this section from the main dining room filled with tables spaced comfortably apart and adorned with floral tablecloths wrapped snugly in clear vinyl. The dining room seats 250 easily, while the bar side accommodates another 150 standing. Jimmy Buffet plays Margaritaville every six to eight weeks. The lineup of Louisiana stars that have performed here include Charmane Neville; her siblings, the Neville Brothers; the popular Cajun group, Evangeline; and Zydeco star Zachary Richard. The restaurant is well known for a menu that is an eclectic blend of New Orleans and the islands: from red beans and rice to Bahamian-style conch chowder to hand-cut fries and key lime pie. This is a fun place, whether you are coming for a meal or an outstanding show.

JAZZ/BLUES/REGGAE:

Palm Court Jazz Café

Location: 1204 Decatur Street
Telephone: 504-525-0200
Clientele: Young/Mature Adult
Format: Jazz
Calendar: Live Entertainment Wed – Sun
Cover/Minimum: Yes/No
Dress: Classy
URL: www.palmcourtjazz.com

Comments: Palm Court Jazz Cafe is the most popular jazz supper club in the French Quarter that exclusively showcases local jazz talent. Founder Nina Buck has worked as a booking agent for jazz tours throughout Europe. Her husband, George Buck, Jr., is one of the United States' key figures in the preservation of jazz, having founded both the Jazzology and GHB record labels. Nina Buck set out to give this club, originally a warehouse, an "old New Orleans" feel when she designed it in 1989. The renovations took almost a year. Danny Barker was the club's first headliner. Palm Court Jazz Café is attractively decorated in wood paneling and bricks against a white background. Several mannequins attired in 1930s fashions are poised throughout the dining room. A display case holds memorabilia associated with the late trumpet virtuoso Bunk Johnson. Lining the walls is a museum-quality collection of photographs of other New Orleans legends such as drummer Milford Dolliole and trombonist Louis Nelson.

Lucien Barabarin and the Sunday Night Swingsters with "Uncle" Lionel Batiste about to sit in.

A host of New Orleans legends played here regularly, including trombonist Louis Nelson leading his own band, the Palm Court Jazz Café Band; the late Dixieland clarinetist and Jazzology recording star Pud Brown; and trumpeter Greg Stafford leading the late Danny Barker's band, the Jazz Hounds. Their current lineup of New Orleans' best include Lucien Barabarin and the Sunday Night Swingsters, Leroy Jones & Katja Toiovla with the Crescent City Joymakers, Lars Edegran with the Palm Court Jazz Band & Jason Marsalis and Otis Bazoon & Leon Brown with the Crescent City Joymakers. Palm Court Jazz Café remains one of the best places in the city to hear New Orleans favorites on a consistent basis. Additionally, their Creole menu features delicious entrees such as creole pasta, red beans & rice with garlic chicken, crawfish nantua flamed in brandy cream sauce and creole beef indienne with mango chutney. Every seat in the dining room offers a good view of the stage. Reservations are strongly encouraged and are the best way to ensure seating near the band.

JAZZ/BLUES/REGGAE:

Preservation Hall

Location: 726 St. Peter Street
Telephone: 504-522-2841
Clientele: Mature Adult
Format: Jazz
Calendar: Live Entertainment Nightly
Cover/Minimum: Yes/No
Dress: Casual
URL: www.preservationhall.com

Comments: Founded in 1961, Preservation Hall is synonymous with the grand tradition of New Orleans jazz. You will have to stand in line at the door, but the short wait is well worthwhile. One of the oldest-running jazz clubs in the French Quarter, the building radiates history and a sense of timelessness. When you enter, you will find a small room with limited seating. Many patrons sit on cushions placed just in front of the band. Others sit on several wooden benches in the middle of the room, while latecomers jockey for a view of the band from the rear. What you get for a mere $10.00 cover is a 30 to 45 minute experience with the Preservation Hall Band, glorious musicians who will have you coming back for more traditional New Orleans jazz night after night. These short sets provide revealing glimpses into the magic of the music to which the city gave birth. Preservation Hall is a must-visit during your stay in New Orleans.

JAZZ/BLUES/REGGAE:

Snug Harbor

Location: 626 Frenchmen Street
Telephone: 504-949-0696
Clientele: Young/Mature Adult
Format: Jazz
Calendar: Live Entertainment Nightly
Cover/Minimum: Yes/No
Dress: Classy
URL: www.snugjazz.com

Comments: Snug Harbor is a beautiful jazz club located at the edge of the French Quarter. The atmosphere is just as the name implies: its several rooms are alcoves giving the illusion of a safe refuge from even the most violent storm. The dining room serves moderately priced seafood and continental cuisine. The jazz room is a two-story gem located at the rear of the building. More than a club, it can be aptly described as a listening room. This is very evident when you watch a show by the soft-spoken pianist Ellis Marsalis. On one visit, I heard him accompanied by his son Jonas on drums and David Polthus on bass. Two Marsalis students, saxophonist Victor Goines and vocalist Roderick Harper, were invited onstage to showcase their talents as well. The audience was as quiet as any I've heard, except during moments when the music became so good,

the interplay between piano, bass and drums so intricate, that affirmation was due in the form of spontaneous applause. Snug Harbor is a key venue for ensuring the continuation of New Orleans' rich jazz heritage. The Ellis Marsalis Trio is featured most Friday evenings. Charmane Neville, the Nicholas Payton Group, and Steve Masakowski and Company have also been regularly featured. A new group of young stars such as prodigy and pianist Nicholas Payton, son of bassist Walter Payton, and Germaine Bazzle, whom the late Snug Harbor owner George Brumet considered the grand dame of New Orleans jazz, are poised to continue in the tradition of Wynton Marsalis and Harry Connick, Jr., both of whom cut their teeth here. Snug Harbor serves dinner from 5:00 p.m. to around midnight. Shows generally consist of two sets, scheduled nightly at 9:00 and 11:00 p.m. Reservations are encouraged for each show. A typical Marsalis performance, for example, will often sell out before 6:00 p.m. Patrons usually begin queuing up about 45 minutes before each show, so get there early.

JAZZ/BLUES/REGGAE:

Sweet Lorraine's Jazz Club

Location: 1931 St. Claude Ave.
Telephone: 504-945-9654
Clientele: Young/Mature Adult
Format: Blues / Jazz
Calendar: Live Entertainment Tues, Thurs, Fri and Sat
Sun Jazz Brunch 11:00 AM – 3:00 PM
Cover/Minimum: Yes/No
Dress: Casual/Classy

Comments: Lorraine Sylvester was no stranger to the hospitality industry, having opened one of her first lounges, Melvina's & Lorraine's Garden of Joy, in 1944 with her mother, Melvina McCarthy. Lorraine and her husband, Paul Sylvester Sr., operated several restaurants and lounges during the 1950s. In 1958, Lorraine ventured out as a sole proprietary when she opened Lorraine's Lounge, followed by several others of the same name in different areas of the city. She opened her last venture, Lorraine's Dugout Lounge, in 1976. When Lorraine passed away in 1984, Paul Sylvester Jr. took over the business and opted to transform his mother's club to a live jazz and supper club venue. He renamed his mother's place Sweet Lorraine's Jazz Club, both a testament to her legacy and the Nat King Cole standard, "Sweet Lorraine." The younger Sylvester, a Saint Augustine HS and Texas Southern University graduate, always had dreams of becoming a world renowned photographer; however, the siren call of a family tradition of entrepreneurship spanning half a century beckoned. To the delight of the surrounding community, he more than answered the call.

Sweet Lorraine's Jazz Club is a cozy supper club located in Faubourg Marigny, just a few blocks northeast of the French Quarter. At first glance, it is the prototypical neighborhood bar. Upon entering, you are greeted by warm wood-panel walls decorated in colorful posters, glass table tops and numerous ceiling fans. The hostess will greet you with a twinkle in her eyes and broad smile. While everyone seems to know each other, a sense of old fashioned Southern hospitality permeates the room. The music is first rate and the ambiance worthy of even the most celebrated jazz rooms. It even has been proclaimed one of the 10 best jazz rooms in America by USA Today. I took in a show by Emile Hall, lead saxophonist for the Irma Thomas, the "Soul Queen of New Orleans." He led a smoking band that excelled on everything from George Benson to Stevie Wonder to Sade. Some of the local and national stars that have performed here include Louisiana Music Hall of Fame inductee Deacon John, the much recorded and sampled pianist Lonnie Liston Smith, Grammy-winning saxophonist Pharoah Sanders, and Argentine sax legend Gato Barbieri.

From left to right: Kurt Brunus on trumpet,
Emile Hall on sax and Warner Williams on keyboard.

Vocalist Michaela Harrison performs each Sunday during brunch while Chucky C. & Clearly Blue are the featured artists for Thursday's "Blues Nite." Weekend acts include artists such as Angela Bell, Clarence Johnson III and Matt Dillion. Sweet Lorraine's is open daily for dinner from 5:00 PM, featuring New Orleans treats such as shrimp or crawfish étouffée, red beans & rice and blackened catfish over spinach.

JAZZ/BLUES/REGGAE:

Tipitina's

Location: 501 Napoleon Ave.
Telephone: 504-895-8477
Clientele: Young/Mature Adult
Format: Blues/Reggae/R&B/Zydeco/Rock & Roll
Calendar: Live Entertainment Nightly
Cover/Minimum: Yes/No
Dress: Casual/Classy
URL: www.tipitinas.com

Comments: Since its inception in 1977, the legendary Tipitina's has been an important venue for New Orleans musicians. In fact, the late Professor Longhair was the inspiration for the club's founders. They wanted a special venue where the legions of Professor Longhair fans could see, hear and experience his magic. At the entrance of Tipitina's, a bronze bust of Henry Roeland Byrd (Professor Longhair's given name) sits poised atop fine granite. Scores of posters from concerts past line the walls near the ceiling: Buckwheat Zydeco, War, Marva Wright, Bobby "Blue" Bland, Bonnie Raitt, and Stanley Jordan, to name a few. The Neville Brothers are a popular monthly attraction. Tipitina's is foremost a dance club. Aside from the stage and two large bars on either side of the first floor, the whole room, devoid of chairs and tables, is a sea of dancers. For some shows, such as a recent performance by native blues star Marva Wright, chairs are set up concert style, ten or so rows deep, nine or so across. Even though the audience gave Wright rapt attention as she belted out her classic blues standards, she entreated her audience to dance because, after all, "this is Tipitina's"! When your appetite grows while dancing the night away or grooving to the beat of blues, jazz, or zydeco rhythms, try the menu featuring New Orleans staples such as jambalaya, gumbo, shrimp and oyster po-boys, or for the adventurous, deep-fried alligator, a dish that many compare to veal or chicken. Tipitina's is a New Orleans institution, a definite must-experience when you are visiting New Orleans.

JAZZ/BLUES/REGGAE:

Vaughan's Lounge

Location: 800 Lesseps St
Telephone: (504) 947-5562
Clientele: Young/Mature Adult
Format: Blues/Jazz
Calendar: Live Entertainment on Thursday Nights
Cover/Minimum: Yes/No
Dress: Casual/Classy

Comments: Vaughan's Lounge has been profiled in the exciting HBO Series, Tremé. The homely appearance outside belies the special treat that awaits inside. It is a "juke joint" that is enormously popular for its laid back atmosphere and the Thursday night performances of local jazz legend and Rebirth Brass Blues Band co-founder, trumpeter Kermit Ruffin and his Barbecue Swingers. When Kermit enters the house, this laid-back atmosphere is transformed. It becomes electrified. Patrons take to the dance floor en masse while others vie for space in front of the band, captivated by the syncopated rhythms of the Barbecue Swingers and Kermit's powerful horn. Window A/C units and ceiling fans provide welcome relief from the summer heat; so does the point and counter-point between Ruffins' trumpet and trombonist Corey Henry as they delve into the music that is uniquely New Orleans. From the traditional "St. James Infirmary" to Rebirth Brass and Blues Band standard, "Do Whatcha Wanna," this band delivers. Take a step outside and you will find a crowd that continues to gather on the club's patio, spilling into this sleepy, Bywater neighborhood street, everyone immersed in the music that envelops all from within. On some evenings, you may even catch a glimpse of icons such as Wynton Marsalis sitting in with the band. Mick Jagger, Kate Hudson, Jude Law and Peter Jennings are among the many celebrities who also have stopped by to see what all the commotion is about. What they find is simple. There's always a Thursday night party here. Seating is limited so you may want to get here early, say around 8:00 PM. The place begins to fill to capacity by 10:00 PM, but there always is room to dance. Chris Songy and Cindy Woods have owned the club since the mid 1980s. They engaged Kermit Ruffin to play there for a family birthday party 18 years ago, and he's been a weekly staple ever since. A neighborhood ordinance permits live entertainment only once per week (Kermit's night), except during the two weeks of the annual New Orleans Jazz Fest. You can then get double your pleasure with performances on Thursday and Friday nights. A visit to New Orleans is not complete without a visit to this enormously popular venue.

DINING

Dooky Chase

Location: 2301 Orleans Street
Telephone: 504-821-0600
Proprietor: The Chase Family
Dress: Casual/Classy
Menu: Creole Cuisine
Price: Modest to Moderate
Hours: Tues – Fri 11:00 AM to 3:00 PM

Comments: When Edgar "Dooky" Chase, Sr. founded this restaurant in 1941, he gave the city a treasure. Dooky Jr. now heads the enterprise, while the family matriarch Leah is the restaurant's head chef and spokesperson. Their Creole and seafood fare is legend throughout Louisiana and much of the country. Patrons of Dooky Chase range from tourists who drop by because they have heard of the restaurant or read Leah Chase's cookbook to old faithfuls who have been customers for decades. The delicious lunch buffet includes fried chicken, breaded veal, smoked sausage, gumbo, red beans and rice, string beans, and French bread. Highlights from the dinner menu are "breast of chicken a la Dooky," stuffed lobster or shrimp, shrimp Creole, crawfish étouffée, and court bouillon. For dessert, try the mouth-watering lemon meringue pie or the praline pudding. Leah Chase is perhaps one of the best-known African American chefs in the United States. She has done cooking segments on local and regional television shows, been featured on the popular Regis and Kathy Lee talk show, and has inspired numerous articles in newspapers and magazines throughout the country. In the course of her career, she has entertained and developed friendships with many of the legends of jazz, R&B, and popular music. Harry Belafonte, Nat King Cole, Bill Eckstine, Duke Ellington, and Sarah Vaughan are names and faces that she recalls easily, guests of the restaurant when Dooky Chase was the most exclusive place in town for African Americans. Former President George W. Bush has dined here. Not to be outdone, President Barack Obama has eaten here twice. Their portraits greet you as you walk through the door. Dooky's remains one of my favorites. You'd have to search high and wide to find a more elegant, down-home dining establishment, especially one with a hostess like Leah Chase. New Orleans cannot be fully appreciated unless you include Dooky's on your list of places to visit. It is unquestionably one of the most outstanding restaurants serving Creole cuisine in the United States.

Dining:

Dunbar's Creole Cuisine (formerly known as Dunbar's Fine Food)

Location: 501 Pine Street, Loyola University Broadway Activities Center
Telephone: 504-861-5451
Proprietor: Celestine Dunbar
Dress: Casual/Classy
Menu: Soul Food, Creole Cuisine
Price: Very Modest
Hours: TBD- Breakfast, Lunch and Dinner Served Daily

Comments: Dunbar's Fine Food enjoys a large following in the Crescent City. On my first visit, it was tucked away in a tiny pink building at 4927 Freret Street, decorated with a poster of the matronly Celestine Dunbar serving a heaping helping of her soulful cuisine, photographs of the Dunbar family and visiting celebrities. The *New Orleans Tribune*, the city's African American monthly, described the restaurant as a New Orleans institution. Dunbar got a late start in the restaurant business, although she has always been an entrepreneur at heart. She was operating a boutique and a beauty salon with her daughter Peggy when the owner of a nearby sandwich shop fell ill and asked Dunbar to run his place in his absence. When he recovered, he no longer wanted the business and sold it to her. The Dunbars operated their first restaurant on Oak Street for two years, and then opted for a better location at 4927 Freret Street. Since the restaurant's modest beginnings in 1989, their business experienced a dramatic increase in popularity; however, the levee failure from the storm waters of Hurricane Katrina proved devastating. Four feet of water caused too much damage and the restaurant closed. Celestine Dunbar and her family evacuated to Eunice, LA for 2 ½ months, then returned. After calling around to universities to inquire about kitchen openings, she got a response that proved to be providential. The Loyola University Law School offered to turn their kitchen over to Dunbar's Fine Foods. She readily accepted. Dunbar still labors to make renovations to their Freret Street eatery, but adversity has led to this new opportunity; e.g., when they finally raise enough capital to re-open Dunbar's on Freret, Celestine Dunbar hopes to continue their contract with the Loyola University Law School Cafeteria. The most popular item on their Freret Street menu, according to Dunbar, were the red beans and rice with fried chicken, mustard greens, and candied yams. Other local favorites included gumbo, turkey necks, stuffed peppers, seafood po-boys, and a spicy rice dish with liver and onions. Law School students and the general public still can experience these wonderful dishes on a rotating basis. Whether you are a student, local resident or tourist, eating a meal at Dunbar's is a special creole and soul food treat; don't forget to save room for their delicious bread pudding or walnut pound cake.

Dunbar's Fine Foods closed in 2014. After more than a year long absence, Gwendolyn Knapp of Nola.Eater.com reported that the restaurant will re-open in early 2016 at 7834 Earhart Blvd. The new restaurant location will be tucked away in an area known as the Gert Town neighborhood, anchored by Xavier University.

DINING:

Lil' Dizzy's Café

Location: 1500 Esplanade Ave
Telephone: 504-569-8997
Proprietor: Wayne Bechet
Dress: Casual
Menu: Creole Cuisine, Soul Food
Price: Modest
Hours: Mon – Sat 7:00 AM – 2:00 PM

Comments: I first met Wayne Bechet at his late father's historic restaurant, Eddie's, in 1993. The food was outstanding. Wayne carries on his father's tradition of great Creole Cuisine and New Orleans style hospitality. The wildly popular HBO series Tremé has given the restaurant much appreciated national exposure by featuring Lil' Dizzy's on one of its episodes. See "Eddie's" in the Hall of Memories section of this book in order to read the history of the Bechet Family in Creole cuisine and jazz.

DINING:

Loretta's Too

Location: 2101 N Rampart St
Telephone: (504) 944-7068
Proprietor: Loretta Harrison
Dress: Casual/Classy
Menu: Praline Candy, Cakes, Pies and Soul Food
Price: Modest
Hours: Tues – Fri 9:00 AM to 5:00 PM
URL: www.lorettaspralines.com

Comments: Loretta Harrison's Praline Booth is a fixture at the annual New Orleans Jazz & Heritage Festival. She answered an ad in 1987 soliciting vendors for Jazz Fest and has been going back time and again. Her booth became the seed experience that led to her establishing a booth at the historic Farmer's Market in the French Quarter. After experiencing tremendous success in the French Quarter, she opened a distribution store/warehouse in the Faubourg Marigny section of the city.

Much more than a store or warehouse, it is a tastefully appointed dining establishment where you can order her fabulous praline candy, cakes and pies. After Hurricane Katrina, hers was one of the first restaurants to reopen, having sustained little to no damage. She served lunch and dinner to appreciative relief workers that had few other options for a home-cooked meal. Her act of charity opened the door for another opportunity, serving delicious soul food and seafood each Friday. On warm summer afternoons, stop by her patio out back and treat yourself to a cool, refreshing New Orleans snow cone.

Dining:

Tee-Eva's Old Fashioned Pies and Pralines

Location: 4430 Magazine St, Uptown
Telephone: 504 899 8350
Proprietor: Eva Louis Perry
Dress: Casual
Menu: Praline Candy, Pies, Creole Cuisine
Price: Moderate
Hours: Vary; Call ahead
URL: www.tee-evapralines.com

Comments: Eva Louis Perry opened her first establishment in 1987, a kitchen from which she sold her delicious pies and pralines to local restaurants and other retail outlets. She moved to her Uptown location in 1994 and has been serving up deep dish pies, pralines and hot gumbo ever since. Her reputation quickly spread throughout New Orleans and her treats have been featured in numerous magazines such as Elle and Home and Garden, as well as television appearances on the Food Network and Travel channels. Her granddaughter now runs the restaurant and continues the tradition that "Tee Eva" originated.

Dining:

The Praline Connection

Location: 542 Frenchman Street
Telephone: 504-943-3934
Proprietor: Cecil Kaigler and Curtis Moore
Dress: Casual/Classy
Menu: Creole/Soul Food/Cajun
Price: Modest
Hours: Mon – Sat, 11:00 AM – 10:00 PM; Sun, 11:00 AM – 9:00 PM
URL: www.pralineconnection.com

Comments: The Praline Connection is one of the most exciting new soul food restaurants to arrive on the New Orleans scene in years. The response since its 1990 grand opening has been overwhelming. The dining room is reminiscent of a French café, with waiters and waitresses attired in black pants, white shirts, and derby hats. The service is Southern hospitality at its best, and the cuisine rates among the city's finest. The smothered pork chips, red beans and rice, collards, and cornbread are mouth-watering. Additional items from their outstanding menu include crawfish or shrimp étoufée, jambalaya, fried, basted or stewed chicken, and mustard and collard greens. The cheesecake with praline sauce highlights a list of delicious desserts. You also must try the praline candy and other treats available in their candy store adjacent to the dining room. Cecil

Kaigler and Curtis Moore spent many coffee breaks during their nearly 18 years at the BP Company, dreaming of opening their own restaurant. After two failed ventures, their third met with success. The Praline Connection has garnered numerous awards and has been featured in local, national and international publications: the *New Orleans Daily*, the *Times-Picayune*, *Elle* magazine, the *New York Times*, and *Bon Appetit*, to name a few. A graduate of Southern University, Curtis Moore was honored by the US Small Business Association as the Minority Small Business Advocate of the Year. The business has been featured in *Black Enterprise* magazine as one of the model small business ventures in the country and listed as one of the top 100 places to eat in America by *Money Magazine*. New Orleans Magazine selected the restaurant as the "Readers Choice" favorite for soul-food cuisine in 1993 and 1994. The Praline Connection also does a bustling catering business. Don't miss The Praline Connection.

Dining:

Willie Mae's Scotch House

Location: 2401 St. Ann Street
Telephone: 504.822.9503
Proprietor: Kerry Seaton
Dress: Casual
Menu: Creole/Soul Food/Cajun
Price: Modest
Hours: Mon-Fri 11am-3pm

Comment: Willie Mae Seaton founded this little kitchen in the late 1940s. It first was something of a neighborhood bar. Her home, an attached duplex, was the source of incredible aromas that bar customers had to find irresistible. Sometime in the late 1950s, the bar gave way to the food by neighborhood acclamation. Willie Mae's Scotch house has been a Tremé neighborhood treasure ever since. Her fried chicken is the stuff of legend, so much so that the James Beard Foundation honored the restaurant with its American Classics award in May 2005. The restaurant exploded in popularity, transitioning from a closely guarded Tremé secret to regional and even national acclaim. Then came Katrina just 4 months later, leaving a decimated restaurant and devastating the home of Willie Mae in its wake. Thanks to a volunteer effort led by the Southern Food Alliance and a host of humanitarian citizens, Willie Mae Seaton's home was restored and the restaurant revived, arising from the ashes like the mythological phoenix. The two-year effort to restore this treasure has been beautifully chronicled by the University of Mississippi's media and documentary projects in a documentary titled *Saving Willie Mae's Scotch House.* It is a must see. The National Education Television Association (NETA) has made it available for distribution throughout most of the country.

There is considerable debate as to whether the shack that Willie Mae Seaton founded serves up the best fried chicken in the world. Having eaten all over the world, from bul goki in Korea to tempura in Japan to goulasch in Berlin, I have my favorites. That being said, Willie Mae's Scotch House is one of the most memorable restaurants that I have experienced anywhere. Her fried chicken easily belongs in the conversation of "best ever." They also serve up some delicious red beans & rice, smothered veal and lima beans that make you want to go back for seconds.

Uncle Lionel Batiste, octogenarian and Brass Band icon; a mentor to today's generation of New Orleans horns

Mardi Gras Indian saunters through the French Quarter

Street Corner Symphony: The French quarter
is all music, all the time.

Keeping the peace down on Bourbon Street

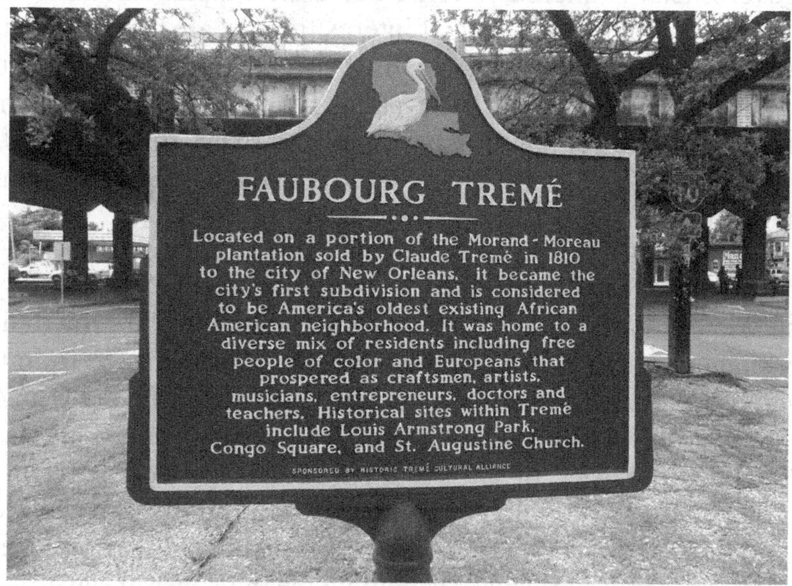

Historic Marker sponsored by the by the Tremé Cultural Alliance

The Tremé Community Center, undergoing restoration

WASHINGTON DC

Washington DC is a study in contrasts. It is the political epicenter of America, housing the executive, legislative and judicial branches of government. Numerous foreign embassies, diplomatic missions, chanceries, lobbyists and special interest groups are arrayed around these seats of power, all jockeying for positions of influence, promoting the interests of their nations, constituents and clients. Amidst this vortex of power resides a citizen's base reported by U.S. Census Bureau 2008 statistics as 54% African American, 40% white American.

African Americans comprised a large percentage of the city's population as early as 1830. Their contributions to the growth and development of our nation's capital have been in evidence from the city's earliest years. Benjamin Banneker, born near Ellicott City, MD in 1731, was a self-taught mathematician and astronomer. In the early 1790s, he participated in the initial survey of the Federal Territory (the emerging Washington DC) by providing daily astronomical observations to project surveyor Andrew Ellicott. He also was one of the first African Americans to articulate the injustices of slavery to a national and international audience through his letters to Secretary of State Thomas Jefferson circa 1791 and the publishing of his Almanacs.

Frederick Douglass was born a slave around 1818 in a small hamlet in Talbot County, MD, some 70 miles east of Washington DC. He was taught to read and write by the age of 12, and soon after was teaching fellow slaves this precious gift. This was one of his earliest acts of public defiance to the institution of slavery. By his early 20s, he had escaped his captors and endeavored on a lifelong and distinguished career as a champion of freedom, advocate of peace, orator, author, diplomat and political activist. He was unarguably one of the most important social and political figures in America's history. In 1877, Douglass purchased a home in Washington DC's Anacostia neighborhood, now known as the Frederick Douglass Historical Site and administered by the National Park Service.

The U.S. Bureau of Refugees, Freedmen, and Abandoned Lands (Freedmen's Bureau) was created by an Act of Congress on March 3, 1865. The Freedmen Bureau's mission, among others, was to aid former slaves through education, employment and health care. Commissioned under the War Department, its director was General Oliver O. Howard, Union Army. In 1867, he co-founded Howard University. The protection offered by the U.S. government to newly freed slaves and the growing stature of Howard University propelled Washington DC into a prominent destination for many African Americans following the Civil War.

Ohio native John A Langford moved to Washington DC in 1902 where he completed the design of the historic "True Reformer Building." During the early 1920s, he was hailed variously as the "Dean of Black Architects" and the Official Architect of the African Methodist Episcopal Church. His landmark designs also include the Chapelle Administrative Building at Allen University (founded in 1870 by the A.M.E. Church).

Mary McLeoud Bethune founded the Daytona Educational and Industrial Training School for Negro Girls in 1904, the genesis for Bethune Cookman University. By 1924, she had taken a second residence in Washington DC, and served as an advisor and confidant of President Franklin D. Roosevelt and Mrs. Eleanor Roosevelt. She founded the National Council of Negro Women (NCNW) in 1935 and served as its President until 1949. The NCNW has been at the forefront of the civil rights movement and the rights of African American women from its inception. The fourth president of this historic organization, Dr. Dorothy I. Height, faithfully served the office for forty years. She strode side by side with Dr. Martin Luther King, blazing the trail of civil rights. In the words of President Barack Obama, "she was the godmother of the civil rights movement."

The promise of an outstanding education offered by Howard University and a secondary education afforded by the Preparatory High School of Colored Youth became a magnet for African Americans throughout the south and the nation. The later became known as the "M Street High School," and now is DC's Dunbar High School. Since its beginning, Howard University has established a track record that makes a strong case for pre-eminence among historically black colleges in America. The list of students, graduates and scholars who have called Howard U their home is vast and distinguished. Imagine walking these hallowed halls and meeting luminaries such as Brigadier General Benjamin O Davis Sr., Poet Paul Laurence Dunbar, former Chief Justice Thurgood Marshall, Nobel Prize Winner Ralph Bunche or former U.N. Ambassador Andrew Young. Award winning actor Ossie Davis, Nobel and Pulitzer Prize-winning author Toni Morrison, the incomparable R&B artists Roberta Flack and Donny Hathaway, and gospel music pioneer Richard Smallwood also are among the many Howard University "treasures of the arts" whose talents were nurtured here.

Three musicians are celebrated in Washington DC as defining artists, their achievements and innovations considered DC's own. The legendary pianist, orchestra leader and composer Edward Kennedy "Duke" Ellington was born here and nurtured his skills in establishments such as those on DC's historic U Street corridor during the 1920s. Recording, composing and performing for more than half a century, he achieved hall of fame status as a jazz innovator, winning national and international acclaim. Singer, songwriter and composer Marvin Gaye enchanted the city, America and the world with his unique vocal style during a career that spanned the 1960s to early 1980s. His music is virtually synonymous with R&B's golden age of the 1960s and 1970s. Gaye's stirring rendition of the National Anthem at the 1983 NBA All Star Game at LA Coliseum will forever remain one of the most powerful and creative interpretations ever recorded. During the early 1970s, Washington DC native Chuck Brown captivated the city, creating a new sound called "go go," uniquely DC and still thriving.

The historic Lincoln Theater on U Street.

Whatever your political persuasion, Washington DC most certainly has something for everyone. The standard tourist attractions, DC monuments and museums, can keep one occupied for an entire visit here. So can a visit planned solely around tours of the White House and other federal complexes. Washington theaters and museums offer adventures in the arts and history that you will find can often be breathtaking.

BEST TOURIST BET FOR THE DOLLAR:

African Cultural Festival each August; Anacostia Museum; Black History National Recreation Trail; Children's Museum; DC Jazz Festival (June); Frederick Douglass Memorial Home; Howard University basketball/football; Georgetown University basketball; University of DC basketball, University of Maryland basketball/football; Memorial Day Jazz Festival; National Air and Space Museum; National Gallery of Art; National Learning Center Capital Children's Museum; national monuments; National Museum of Natural History; Smithsonian Castle and museums (including the Museum of African Art); tours of the Capitol; the spring Cherry Blossom Festival; DC United soccer; Washington Wizards basketball; Washington Redskins football, Washington Capitals hockey; Warner Theater concerts.

JAZZ/BLUES/REGGAE:

BETHESDA BLUES & JAZZ SUPPER CLUB

LOCATION: 7719 Wisconsin Avenue
TELEPHONE: (240) 330-4500
CLIENTELE: Mature Adult
FORMAT: Jazz/Blues/R&B
CALENDAR: Live Performances Nightly
COVER/MINIMUM: Yes/Yes
DRESS: Business Casual/Classy
URL: www.bethesdabluesjazz.com/

COMMENTS: Bethesda Blues & Jazz Supper Club is one of the Washington DC Metro Area's newest and most exciting venues for blues, jazz and R&B. Add to that, a first class dining experience in an intimate setting and you have the prefect ingredients for a fabulous evening of entertainment. The supper club is sited in an historic building that dates back to the late 1930's, originally christened as the Boro Theatre. Owner Rick Brown converted this fabled theatre into a supper club in 2013. His roots run deep in the music and hospitality industry, having been raised by a jazz drummer and a restaurateurs' daughter. Artists who have performed here include Brandord Marsalis, The Intruders & Shawn Allen, The Clayton Brothers, The Nighthawks, The Tom Principato Band With Horns and more. I recently took in a stirring performance by Janiva Magness, two time Blues Music Award "Contemporary Blues Female Artist of the Year" and The Blues Foundation's "B.B. King Entertainer of the Year" in 2009. She and the … Supper Club presented a benfit performance for the "Child Welfare League of America," one of the oldest national children's advocacy organizations in America. An alumnus of the foster care system, Janiva Magness weaved stories of her experiences as an "at risk youth" while soulfully delivering the blues. It was an evening well spent and a first class display of 'giving back" by Magness and the Bethesda Blues and Jazz Supper Club.

JAZZ/BLUES/REGGAE:

BLUES ALLEY

LOCATION: 1073 Wisconsin Ave. N.W.
TELEPHONE: (202) 337-4141
CLIENTELE: Mature Adult
FORMAT: Jazz/Blues/R&B
CALENDAR: Live Performances Nightly
COVER/MINIMUM: Yes/Yes
DRESS: Casual/Classy
URL: www.Bluesalley.com

COMMENTS: Blues Alley is one of the premier jazz supper clubs in the United States. Opened in 1972, it has long attracted jazz aficionados from throughout the country and abroad. Virtually every notable jazz entertainer of the modern era has performed here. My first experience at Blues Alley came in 1983 when I was enthralled for an evening by the sultry sounds of the late Eartha Kitt, legendary actress, jazz vocalist and cabaret star. The late Sarah Vaughn and Nancy Wilson are two other mistresses of jazz who have performed here. The list of other jazz greats who have graced this historic venue reads like a hall of fame journal: Dizzy Gillespie, Maynard Ferguson and Ramsey Lewis to name just a few more. The club has also featured blues artist such as the late blues guitarist and singer

Albert Collins, blues pioneer Buddy Guy as well as R&B notables such as Harold Melvin and Jerry Butler. Blues Alley also features top flight entertainment that showcases Washington DC artists such as the venerable "go go" pioneer Chuck Brown, DC fusion stars The Blackbirds, and innovative Jazz / R&B / Rap pioneers, The Marcus Johnson Project. Blues Alley is located in the heart of Washington's famous Georgetown district. In addition to the entertainment, Blues Alley also offers an exciting menu that includes a fantastic array of seafood, steaks and Creole cuisine. In 1985, Blues Alley and the late trumpet master Dizzy Gillespie founded the Blues Alley Jazz Society. This non-profit venture has resulted in a fantastic educational opportunity for numerous Washington DC children who are disenfranchised, to experience jazz, learn from the masters and even pursue careers in the arts. The organization has partnered with other organizations such as the National Park Service, the National Endowment for the Arts, and the Smithsonian Institution to help accomplish these objectives. Blues Alley is truly one of Washington DC's most inviting attractions and a must-see during your stay here.

JAZZ/BLUES/REGGAE:

Bohemian Caverns

LOCATION: 2001 11 St NW (Corner of U St and 11th)
TELEPHONE: (202) 299-0800
CLIENTELE: Mature Adult
FORMAT: Jazz/Blues/R&B
CALENDAR: Live Performances Vary
COVER/MINIMUM: Yes/Yes
DRESS: Casual/Classy
Status: CLOSED

COMMENTS: In 1926, this fabled venue opened its doors as the Club Caverns. It was almost immediately one of DC's most important entertainment venues, a place where Washingtonians dressed in their finest were enthralled by the likes of Duke Ellington and his magnificent orchestra and Cab Calloway strutting in White Tuxedo, delighting everyone with his call and response to "Minnie the Moocher." Between 1950 and early 1960, the club changed its name to the Crystal Caverns, then Bohemian Caverns. The Caverns became increasingly popular. It was a must stop on America's fabled "Chittlin Circuit." Billie Holiday would enchant all with her incomparable voice, rendering lyrics to "Good Morning Heartache" and the haunting "Strange Fruit" in a manner that stayed with you always. Ramsey

Lewis recorded his critically acclaimed album, Live At the Bohemian Caverns in 1962. John Coltrane, Miles Davis, Roberta Flack and the Supremes also were among the constellation of stars in jazz and R&B who have performed here. The club continued to enjoy success until the riots of 1968, a period that signaled the decline of many U Street venues. Bohemian Caverns was purchased and reopened by Amir Afshar in 1998, emerging as an important element in the Revitalization of U Street. Omrao Brown and two other partners purchased the club in 2006. They have undertaken a major renovation of Bohemian Caverns, revamping all three levels to create an even more versatile entertainment experience, but maintaining its historic character as one of DC's most important jazz venues. Omrao serves as managing partner and books the local, national and international acts. He and his brother, Sashi, owe much of their love and passion to jazz to their father, Northeastern University Professor and jazz saxophonist Leonard Brown. You can hear their father at Bohemian Caverns on occasion, as well as current jazz legends such as Ron Carter, bassist extraordinaire, the incomparable Wynton Marsalis and the newly formed Bohemian Caverns Orchestra. Bohemian Caverns features jazz on the lower level, the upscale restaurant Mahogany on the main and "Liv," a contemporary music and dance venue on the upper level.

JAZZ/BLUES/REGGAE:

Columbia Station

LOCATION: 2325 18th NW
TELEPHONE: (202) 462-6040
CLIENTELE: Young/Mature Adult
FORMAT: Blues/Jazz
CALENDAR: Live Performances Mon to Thur and Weekends
COVER/MINIMUM: No/Yes
DRESS: Casual/Classy
URL: www.columbiastationdc.com

COMMENTS: A very nice restaurant to experience a jazz or blues performance. There aren't many places that offer great music without a cover. When you are in the Adams Morgan neighborhood, this is a must-visit. Open daily for dinner from 5 PM Tues to Thu and 4 PM on weekends, they offer menu choices that range from burgers to steaks to an interesting Cajun mix that includes blackened shrimp, mussels and sausage, served with black beans and sauce. The Peter Elderman Quintet are a fixture most Sundays, hosting a

A sizzling jam session featuring Web Grant on drums, Bill "Magic" Lavender-Bey on upright, Rob Pasternek on piano and promising saxophonist Michael Brandon

jam session that begins at 4 PM and performance beginning at 8:30 PM. The Third Truth Trio and the Ben Young Quartet also are featured Tuesday and Thursday nights respectively. The Butch Warren Experience provides an even more compelling reason to drop in at Columbia Station. Butch Warren, upright bassist, is one of the area's best kept secrets; however, jazz historians will recall that he recorded with some of the legends of Blue Note records during the early 1960s, artists such as Donald Byrd on his album "Free Form" in 1961, Dexter Gordon on his album "Go!" in 1962 and Joe Henderson's "Page One" in 1963. Warren toured for several months during the early 1960s with the late jazz master and bebop pioneer, Thelonious Monk, and was featured on his album "It's Monk's Time" on the Columbia Label in 1964. You can catch the Butch Warren Experience every Wednesday night beginning at 8:30 PM and during their 4:00 PM jam sessions each Saturday followed by an evening performance around 8:30 PM. Come early for the ambiance, stay for an evening of outstanding jazz.

JAZZ/BLUES/REGGAE:

HR-57 Center for the Preservation of Jazz and Blues

LOCATION: 816 H St N.E Previously Located @ 1610 14th St. N.W.
TELEPHONE: (202) 253-0044
CLIENTELE: Mature Adults
FORMAT: Jazz
CALENDAR: Live Jazz Weds thru Saturday
Jam Sessions Each Wednesday and Thursday
COVER/MINIMUM: Yes/No
DRESS: Casual/Classy
Status: CLOSED

COMMENTS: In 1987, the United States Congress passed House Concurrent Resolution 57, a measure that was sponsored by Congressman John Conyers, Jr. and designated jazz as a "national American treasure." The founder of HR-57, Tony Puesan, considered this resolution a perfect name for his new jazz venue, an establishment in DC's historic U Street corridor dedicated to the preservation of jazz and blues. The club is located in one of those historic Washington DC row houses. Constructed in 1890, the small lot size of 3000 square feet belies the footprint of the building which is quite large, more than 6,100 square feet on two levels. Given the historic character of the building, the club's décor is very much in harmony; brick walls, wood floors and bric a brac ceiling painted black give the club an understated elegance. The foyer and main level are lined with tables, sofas and a wood bar, the area of choice for patrons who want to hear the music while engaging in quiet discourse with companions. Step down into the concert room and the seating is cozy with the stage, an elevated bandstand with a black back drop accented by the club's logo, HR-57, in white. This is the area for listening, for becoming one with the music. The Antonio Parker Quartet, AJ Parham (jazz vocals), Saltman Knowles (bassist), and Jimmy Jackson Quartet are among their regularly featured artists. Eric Lewis (ELEW) also packs the house whenever he is in town. ELEW is an innovative pianist who has broken new ground by fusing jazz with rock, creating a genre that he calls "RockJazz." You can catch a show here for anywhere from $8 to $23. Many young, hip locals consider this the place of choice for impressing on that first date; especially owing to the modest cover and the opportunity to bring one's favorite bottle of red for a very modest $3 corking fee. I simply consider HR-57 to be one of Washington DC's best kept secrets, an outstanding jazz club that harkens back to the days when you could hear Harlem Renaissance quality music in the most intimate of settings.

JAZZ/BLUES/REGGAE:

Lincoln Theater

LOCATION: 1215 U St. N.W.
TELEPHONE: (202) 328-6000
CLIENTELE: Mature Adults
FORMAT: Musicals, Theater, Blues, R&B, Jazz and more…
CALENDAR: Performances Vary
COVER/MINIMUM: Yes/ N/A
DRESS: Casual/Classy/Evening Wear
URL: thelincolntheatre.org

COMMENTS: The Lincoln Theater is the centerpiece of Washington DC's renovation of the historic U Street corridor. It was constructed in 1921 and held its grand opening the following year. From its inception, the Lincoln Theater became a focal point for the arts among Washington DC's African American community. Initially serving as a venue for theatrical and vaudeville productions, the theater also emerged as one of the most important music halls on the east coast for experiencing live performances that included R&B, Blues and Jazz. Washington DC's favorite son Duke Ellington, Ella Fitzgerald, Cab Calloway, Pearl Bailey, Louie Armstrong and Billie Holiday led a long parade of stars that performed here dating back to the Harlem Renaissance and beyond. Post renovation stars (since

1993) have included Wynton Marsalis, DC's own Chuck Brown and comedian and activist Dick Gregory. The Lincoln Theater kicked off the summer of 2010 by presenting the musical "Duke Ellington's Sophisticated Ladies." The performances were so compelling and entertaining that the musical was held over by popular demand. The Lincoln Theater has been elegantly restored. It provides plus seating for 1295 patrons in an environment that dazzles. It is as precious to Washington DC as a Ming vase, but unlike the storied Chinese treasure, this is a jewel that the whole family can and must experience

JAZZ/BLUES/REGGAE:

TAKOMA STATION Tavern

LOCATION: 6914 4TH ST. N.W.
TELEPHONE: (202) 829-1999
CLIENTELE: Mature/Young Adult
FORMAT: Jazz, Blues, Reggae, Comedy
CALENDAR: Live Performances Vary
COVER/MINIMUM: Yes/Yes
DRESS: Casual/Classy
URL: www.takomastation.com

COMMENTS: Takoma Station is one of the Washington area's most popular jazz clubs. It features great acoustics and an intimate environment for experiencing some of the hot young jazz talent that the area produces. The atmosphere is both warm and intimate, from the hardwood floors to the cozy bench seating to the photos and prints depicting some of the legends of jazz that adorn the walls. While you're being entertained by the syncopated rhythms of jazz, you can enjoy a varied menu that includes crab cake platters, stuffed shrimp, and filet mignon. Takoma Station was founded in 1984 and has enjoyed a growing following over the years. The late Bernard Shaw, Takoma Park resident and award-winning CNN correspondent, considered this establishment to be his favorite jazz club. Legendary musicians sometimes drop in to see what all the fuss is about, leading to surprise visits by such stars as Gil Scott Heron, Stevie Wonder, Miles Davis and Wynton Marsalis. The club normally features live entertainment five nights a week, Wednesday through Sunday: local favorites such as Spur of the Moment, Chuck Brown, Maiesha Rashad and Mary Ann Redmond. Takoma Station is an establishment that you definitely want to visit when touring the Washington area.

JAZZ/BLUES/REGGAE:

The Birchmere Music Hall

LOCATION: 3701 Mt. Vernon Ave, Alexandria, VA
TELEPHONE: (703) 549-7500
CLIENTELE: Young / mature adults
FORMAT: Jazz, Blues, Classical, Pop and more
CALENDAR: Live Performances Vary
COVER/MINIMUM: Yes/No
DRESS: Business Casual/Classy
URL: www.birchmere.com

Comments: The Birchmere has been a major presenter of entertainment in the Washington DC area for over three decades. It is a nationally and internationally acclaimed concert hall. With seating for more than 500, it is one of the larger settings that afford an evening of live entertainment while dining and, on some occasions, dancing. Recent performances were highlighted by such artists as ten time Grammy winner Bobby McFerrin, master of vocals, jazz improvisation and conductor; New Orleans ambassadors of R&B and soul, the Neville Brothers; Alex Bugnon, jazz pianist; and two-time Grammy winner Joan Armatrading, folk and blues star. The fall and winter calendar for 2010 features a great lineup that includes McCoy Tyner (jazz pianist, recipient of four Grammy Awards and National Endowment for the Arts Jazz Master) and the McCoy Tyner Quartet;

blues guitarist and co-founder of the Nighthawks, Jimmy Thackery; and R&B star / composer / producer Kenneth Brian "Babyface" Edmonds. Entertainment offerings of The Birchmere Music Hall are varied and exciting. While being enthralled by your favorite singer or musician, you also can dine on a menu that includes catfish with red beans & rice, Cajun gumbo, crab & shrimp Creole, Texas barbecue brisket, beignets with raspberry sauce and more.

JAZZ/BLUES/REGGAE:

The Kennedy Center Jazz Club (KC Jazz Club)

Panoramic views from the Terrace Rooftop at the Kennedy Center
LOCATION: 2700 F Street, NW
TELEPHONE: (202) 467-4600
CLIENTELE: All Ages
FORMAT: Jazz
CALENDAR: Performances Vary
COVER/MINIMUM: Yes/No
DRESS: Casual, Classy, Chic
URL: www.kennedy-center.org

Comments: The Kennedy Center for the Performing Arts opened its doors in 1971. It is an exquisite memorial to President John Fitzgerald Kennedy and the "torch bearer" for performing arts in America. The center is maintained and operated through funding by the federal government; however, live performances are sustained through ticket sales and corporate sponsorships. Venues within the Kennedy Center include the 2,400-seat Concert Hall, its Opera House that seats around 2,300, the Eisenhower Theatre (for ballet, small operas, musicals, and dance) with 1,100 seats and the Terrace Theatre where intimate performances can accommodate about 500 guests. The Concert Hall and the center's Terrace Gallery are the largest venues in Washington DC where top local, national and international jazz musicians are featured throughout the year. It also is an important resource for jazz education, the preservation of jazz, and promotion of jazz as an American art form. Dr. Billy Taylor, legendary pianist composer and educator, has served as the Kennedy Center's Artistic Director for Jazz since 1994. The KC Jazz Club is an intimate, cabaret-style venue situated in the Kennedy Center's roof level, Terrace Gallery. The acoustics are unrivalled, the ambiance of the room elegant and warm. The various venues within the Kennedy Center, whether it is the Concert Hall, Millennium Stage, Terrace Theatre or intimate KC Jazz Club offer an opportunity to experience legends across the spectrum of jazz. Among them have been scintillating performances such as the tenor / contralto voice of Jimmy Scott or the straight ahead stylings of saxophonist Jimmy Heath, or the piano riffs of Arturo O'Farill, Jr., son of the late Latin jazz pioneer Arturo "Chico" O'Farill. The concert schedule for performances is posted on the Kennedy Center website and provides a great opportunity to plan visits up to a year in advance. For example, a trip to the nation's capital a few years past featured great gifts for one's Christmas stocking, the Preservation Hall Jazz Band presenting their "Creole Christmas," followed by New Year's Eve with The Jon Faddis Jazz Orchestra of New York and Grammy nominee Nnenna Freelon.

JAZZ/BLUES/REGGAE:

The Music Center at Strathmore

LOCATION: 5301 Tuckerman Ln, Bethesda, MD
TELEPHONE: (202) 829-1999
CLIENTELE: All Ages
FORMAT: Jazz, Blues, Classical, Pop and more
CALENDAR: Live Performances Vary
COVER/MINIMUM: Yes/No
DRESS: Business Casual/Classy
URL: www.strathmore.org

COMMENTS: Captain James Frederick Oyster and his wife purchased 99 acres of land in 1899 and laid the foundation for this historic mansion. It was variously owned by inventor and baking industry innovator, Charles Corby, St. Mary's Academy and the American Speech-Language-Hearing Association. The mansion and remaining property consisting of 11 acres was deeded to Montgomery County in 1979, was renamed Strathmore Hall and dedicated as the county's first center for the arts. The Music Center at Strathmore, a concert hall and education center with seating for up to 1976 patrons was constructed in 2001. It has since become a major concert venue for national and internationally acclaimed artists as well as an incubator for launching the careers of local artists. Strathmore has an incredible array of partners such as the Baltimore Philharmonic orchestra, National Philharmonic, Washington Performing Arts Society and the Levine School of Music. Each of their partners provides invaluable educational opportunities for the community and fabulous entertainment across the spectrum of the arts. This is a special venue for special events. Strathmore's 2010 – 2011 calendar featured classical and jazz pianist Rachel Franklin, Matt Belzer on Sax and bassist Mike Formanek, exploring the links between classical and jazz music; An Evening of Jazz and Jobim with Ron Kearns, saxophone and Paul Wingo, guitarist, two Baltimore-Washington jazz greats; and Blues guitarist Jef Lee Johnson.

JAZZ/BLUES/REGGAE:

The Zoo Bar Café

LOCATION: 3000 Connecticut Ave. NW
TELEPHONE: (202) 232-4225
CLIENTELE: Young / Mature Adults
FORMAT: Blues, Jazz
CALENDAR: Live Entertainment Thursday - Sunday
COVER/MINIMUM: No/No
DRESS: Casual, Classy
Status: CLOSED

Comments: Located directly across the street from the Washington National Zoo, the Zoo Bar Café is on the very short list of Washington DC clubs whose primary focus is blues as well as jazz. Mike Flaherty and the Dixieland Direct Jazz Band can be heard most Sunday evenings. The club's monthly lineup also has featured artists such as Sookey Jump Blues Band delivering New Orleans flavored zydeco, R&B and blues and the scintillating "jump blues" of Flatfoot Sam, a widely travelled musician who has performed with the likes of Clarence "Gatemouth" Brown, Koko Taylor, Junior Wells, and Charlie Musselwhite. The Open Mic Blues Jam with Big Boy Little has become a staple for aspiring musicians each Thursday evening.

JAZZ/BLUES/REGGAE:

TWINS Jazz

LOCATION: 1344 U Street, NW (top floor)
TELEPHONE: (202) 234-0072
CLIENTELE: Young/Mature Adult
FORMAT: Jazz
CALENDAR: Live Performances Weds-Sun
COVER/MINIMUM: Yes/Yes
DRESS: Casual/Classy
URL: www.twinsjazz.com

COMMENTS: Kelly and Maze Tesfaye decided to open their jazz club after attending the University of the District of Columbia in 1987. Having supplemented her tuition by working part-time in restaurants, Kelly decided that one could open a small jazz club and still be profitable. Theirs was a risk that has paid dividends many times over. Twins is as cozy and intimate a little hideaway as you will find.

I had the pleasure of experiencing the sizzling piano virtuoso, Kenny Drew, on my first evening here. Performances at Twins are especially engaging because the seating is so close to the stage that the sensation of being a part of the performance is assured. Twins also offers a menu that highlights Ethiopian, Haitian-Caribbean and continental cuisine.

DINING:

Anacostia Cafeteria

LOCATION: 1123 Howard RD SE
TELEPHONE: (202) 678-7850
PROPRIETOR: United House of Prayer for All People
DRESS: Casual
MENU: Soul Food
PRICE: Modest
HOURS: Mon – Thur, 7:00 AM- 5:00 PM, Fri, 7:00 AM – 7:00 PM, Sat – Sun, 8:00 AM – 6:00 PM

COMMENTS: The Anacostia Cafeteria is a smaller version of its sister cafeteria, Saint's Paradise, in Northwest DC. While the latter serves the National Headquarters Church, the smaller Anacostia Cafeteria has become a staple of DC's Anacostia community. Locals affectionately call it "Daddy Grace," after the charismatic founder, Bishop Charles M. "Sweet Daddy" Grace. It also is located in the basement of the United House of Prayer for All People. The iconic Barry Farms basketball court, a favorite stop for current and former NBA basketball players each summer, is located just a block away. Also unique to this congregation is the Sweet Heaven Kings, a 16-member gospel brass and percussion band that has achieved regional as well as national acclaim.

Members of the engineering staff at Washington DC's *Botanical Gardens* consider the Anacostia Cafeteria their "go to move." When John Griffin announces that he is "going to the Church," staff members quickly place their orders, the most favored menu items consisting of smothered pork chops and turkey wings. I took two dinners to my colleagues at Long & Foster consisting of barbecued ribs, fried chicken, mac & cheese, collard greens, string beans, candied yams and corn bread. Expecting to find only a couple of co-workers on a late afternoon weekday, word quickly spread and these two meals were consumed in a flash. Comments ranged from "awesome to amazing to we want to place orders when you go again." Be sure to stop by and see why Anacostia residents keep coming back for more.

DINING:

Ben's Chili Bowl

LOCATION: 1213 U Street NW
TELEPHONE: (202) 667-0909
PROPRIETOR: The Ali Family
DRESS: Casual/Classy Next Door
MENU: Ben's Famous Chili Dogs, half smokes and such

PRICE: Modest
HOURS: Mon thru Thurs- 6:00 AM – 2:00 AM
Fri- 6:00 AM – 4:00 AM; Sat- 7:00 AM – 4:00 AM;
Sun- 11:00 AM – 11:00 PM
URL: www.benschilibowl.com

Comments: Ben's Chili Bowl is a Washington DC institution, founded by the late Ben Ali and his wife Virginia in 1958. Located on the city's historic U Street, Washingtonians claim it as their own, a "must see and experience" venue right up there with Washington's historic monuments. The restaurant has endeared itself to Washington DC for many reasons. While millions of fans adore their famous "half smokes," DC residents are especially grateful to founders Ben & Virginia Ali for keeping their restaurant afloat during one of the most difficult periods in DC history—the collapse of U Street as a vital economic engine following the riots of 1968 and during the neighborhood upheaval caused by the construction of the city's Metro stations. Their steadfastness secured Ben's Chili Bowl as an anchor for the future revitalization of U Street. In 2004, Ben's Chili Bowl was one of four restaurants in America that were given the James Beard Foundation America's Classics Award. Their awards are considered preeminent among restaurants, lauded by Time magazine as "the Oscars of the food world." Celebrities from around the world have eaten here; as have heads of state, President Barack Obama foremost among them. On the 10th of January, 2009, just ten days before being sworn in as the 44th President of the United States, President Obama and Washington DC Mayor Adrian Fenty paid a surprise visit. After all, Mayor Fenty famously advised, "in order to know Washington DC, you have to go to Ben's Chili Bowl." The popularity of Ben's can easily be observed as you drive by. Folks from around the world are always gathered at the restaurant's front door, eagerly chatting and waiting in line for a great chili dog, half smoke or milk shake. Come for the glorious chili and smokes, stay and be immersed in historic ambiance.

DINING:

Ben's Next Door Bar & Restaurant

LOCATION: 1213 U Street NW
TELEPHONE: (202) 667-0909
PROPRIETOR: The Ali Family
DRESS: Casual/Classy Next Door
MENU: Southern and Continental Cuisine
PRICE: Modest
HOURS: Mon thru Thur- 11:00 AM – 2:00 AM
Fri and Sat- 11:00 AM – 3:00 AM;
Sun- 11:00 AM – 2:00 AM
URL: www.bensnextdoor.com

Comments: Ben's Next Door occupies the building adjacent Ben's Chili Bowl. The restaurant's name is an understatement. The Next Door Bar & Restaurant is one of Washington's best kept secrets; a restaurant and sports bar that provides an ideal atmosphere for watching local sports such as Washington Capitals hockey, Wizards basketball, Redskins football or DC United soccer. Ten flat screen TVs are strategically place throughout. The restaurant also offers an outstanding menu featuring starter dishes such as mini sliders (crab, filet, or combo, served on mini potato buns with onion straws and remoulade sauce) and entrées that include tasty morsels of sautéed shrimp & organic white grits, brine fried chicken or crispy skin salmon with "perfect" mashed potatoes and sautéed spinach. Where Ben's Chili Bowl offers down home ambiance, Next Door contrasts by providing a very modern dining experience with the promise of an expanding live entertainment option. Tuesday evenings feature top metro DC area musicians in a lineup that has included "alternative soul" pianist/vocalist Terrence Cunningham, the versatile jazz, R&B, gospel, and hip hop vocalist Lauren White, and R&B / "neo-soul" vocalist Wendy McIntyre. The Next Door restaurant & bar, like its parent, Ben's Chili Bowl, is very much a family affair. Two of Ben & Virginia Ali's sons, Kamal and Nazim, run the day-to-day operations. They also oversee the family's Kiosks at Washington Nationals baseball games, another venture that affords Nationals baseball fans and visiting teams to experience the magic that Ben & Virginia created when they first envisioned their "half smokes."

DINING:

FLORIDA AVENUE GRILL

LOCATION: 1100 Florida Ave. N.W.
TELEPHONE: (202) 265-1586
PROPRIETOR: Imar Hutchins
DRESS: Casual
MENU: Soul Food
PRICE: Very Modest
HOURS: Tues-Sat/ 8:00 AM-8:00 PM
URL: www.Floridaavenuegrill.com

COMMENTS: Mr. & Mrs. Lacey Wilson Sr. came to Washington by way of Burlington N.C. They founded the Florida Avenue Grill in 1944. Lacey Sr. built the business and staked his reputation on good food and fast service, a quality that endeared the Wilson restaurant to its primary clientele, DC taxi drivers, as World War II wound down. Lacey Jr. took over the family business in 1974. The restaurant and surrounding property were purchased by Morehouse College and Yale Law School graduate Imar Hutchins circa 2005. A prominent Washington Attorney and real estate developer, Hutchins converted the adjacent parking lot to an elegant 26 unit condominium complex, appropriately named the Lacey, and has ably carried on the tradition started by the Wilson family. The Florida Avenue Grill now has expanded their base of loyal patrons to a national following. The longevity of this landmark institution is a testament to the quality of service provided here. Located about two blocks from Howard University, it is the "flagship" of Washington DC's soul food establishments. How popular is this restaurant? When you walk in, take a look at the autographed portrait photos above the counter—they're photos of celebrities who have dined here. Clint Eastwood, Natalie Cole, Rev. Joseph Lowery, and Charles Barkley are but a few of the luminaries who found their way to this modest, but splendid restaurant. It is "down home cooking" in the middle of the nation's capital. I feasted on a bountiful portion of liver & onions, collard greens and rice. Other items from the menu include, barbecue beef, smothered pork chops, chitterlings, ham hocks and fillet of fresh fried fish. Homemade desserts include bread pudding and peach cobbler. You will also find the Florida Avenue Grill is an excellent choice for breakfast. Try the Chef's Special that features country ham n' eggs, red eye gravy, grits, fried apples or home fries, hot biscuit and coffee. Applauded by the Washingtonian Magazine as a perennial "best cheap eat," this is one of Washington's monuments that you can't leave the city without visiting.

DINING:

GEORGIA BROWN'S

LOCATION: 950 15th St. N.W.
TELEPHONE: (202) 393-4499
PROPRIETOR: Capitol Management Group
DRESS: Casual / Classy
MENU: "Low Country" Cuisine
PRICE: Moderate-Expensive
URL: www.gbrowns.com

COMMENTS: Georgia Brown's is a swank restaurant located in the heart of downtown Washington. There are a number of things that set this restaurant apart. While the focus of this book regarding dining establishments has been predominantly soul food restaurants, I chose to write about Georgia Brown's because it features low country / southern cuisine, a sophisticated cousin to soul food, more closely related to Creole Cuisine, and their very popular "Jazz Brunch." South Carolina's coastal areas are rich in seafood and their legacy of cuisine is infused with seafood dishes transformed by African and Spanish influences. Georgia Brown takes this concept one step further by creating a memorable dining experience that is both elegant and warm. Their concept is unique and has few peers in the Mid-Atlantic Region of the United States. The ambiance of Georgia Brown's is everything one would expect from a restaurant considered one of the best of any kind in Washington DC. They've taken great care to achieve a beautiful interior by commissioning one of the area's top Designers, Adam Tifany, to create a dining room that flows with curved lines, discreet little private alcoves and soft pastels. A sculpture that reminds one of a canopy sprawls along the ceiling, intended to create the illusion of southern magnolia trees and hanging moss. The restaurant's menu is an outstanding compliment to the quality of Tifany's interior design. Executive Chef Jim Foss weaves low country (South Carolina) recipes with nouvelle culinary techniques. The result is masterful. Whatever your pleasure, Georgia Brown's offers several outstanding menu choices that include such dishes as South Carolina-inspired crispy fried Chincoteague Oysters, Charleston She-Crab Soup, smoked salmon "pate," Low Country Shrimp & Grits, and cornmeal-crusted catfish fingers. You also will enjoy their more traditional Southern menu items such as Southern fried chicken, roasted duck a la orange, sugar and spice pork loin, and, among their vegetarian options, black eyed pea cakes. It all goes well with a refreshing glass of orange flavored iced tea. While you're savoring the cuisine at Georgia Brown's, on weekdays and evenings you will hear soft Blues and Jazz piped over the music system. On Saturday nights, Blues performances by regional acts are the norm. Their Sunday Jazz Brunch is also widely popular. Long time wait staffers identify Former President Bill Clinton with his favorite entrée. Our First Lady, Michelle Obama, has twice ordered her "favorite" entrée here. In the interest of executive privacy, I won't share. This is **the** place where Washington DC comes together. From blue collar workers to Congressmen, many have come to call Georgia Brown's their own.

DINING:

Henry's Deli

LOCATION: 1704 U St. N.W.
TELEPHONE: (202) 265-3366
PROPRIETOR: Henry Smith
DRESS: Casual
MENU: Soul Food
PRICE: Very Modest
HOURS: Mon-Thur 10:30 AM- 8:00 PM;
Fri-Sat 10:30 AM-10:00 PM
URL: www.henryssoulcafe.com

COMMENTS: Henry Smith opened Henry's Deli on U Street in 1967. His family has been serving up soulful dishes of fried chicken, mac & cheese, meatloaf and collards to an ever appreciative Washington. What they really hang their hats on, though, is mouthwatering sweet potato pie; in fact, Washingtonians stand in line during the days preceding Thanksgiving in order to bring these delicious concoctions home. It is such a tradition for some families that guests will say upon arrival for Thanksgiving dinner, "I just know you got one of those pies from Henry's."

DINING:

Henry's Soul Café

LOCATION: 5431 Indian Head Hwy, Oxon Hill, MD
TELEPHONE: (301) 749-6856
PROPRIETOR: Jermaine Smith and Bernard Brooks, Jr.
DRESS: Casual
MENU: Soul Food
PRICE: Very Low
HOURS: Mon 11:30 AM-7:00 PM; Tues-Sat 11:30 AM- 9:00 PM; Sunday 12:00 PM-8:00 PM
URL: www.henryssoulcafe.com

COMMENTS: Jermaine Smith learned the restaurant trade from his father, Henry Smith, by helping out at the family's deli on U Street. Over the years, what he perceived as chores became an apprenticeship, planting the seed and nurturing of a second-generation entrepreneur. Jermaine and longtime friend Bernard Brooks, Jr. transported the Henry's Deli concept to Oxon Hill, MD in 1997. Jermaine's sister, Henrietta Smith-Davis, serves as manager of operations. The restaurant offers the same smorgasbord of soul food as Henry's Deli, including the "best pie on the planet," their sweet potato pie. Jermaine and Bernard have taken the concept even further by offering a "sweet potato pie kit," online at henryssweetpotatopie.com. The management team boasts annual restaurant pie sales of 50,000 or more. Given their success to date, Jermaine, Henrietta and Bernard hope to expand their concept as franchises nationwide.

DINING:

Horace & Dickey's Seafood Carryout

LOCATION: 809 12th St. N.E.
TELEPHONE: (202) 390-6040
PROPRIETOR: Richard Shannon
DRESS: Casual
MENU: Seafood, Soul Food
PRICE: Modest
HOURS: Mon-Sat 10:00 AM- 2:00 AM; Sun 10:00 AM-9:00 PM

COMMENTS: Everyone describes this carryout as "a hole in the wall." The description is deserved. Don't visit if you are looking for ambiance, come for the mouth-watering fish sandwiches. During the late 1940s, this location was the home of another seafood joint, Boyd's Seafood, a DC landmark that achieved "urban legend" status among long time locals who reminisce that their fish sandwiches were "to die for." Horace & Dickey's Seafood Carryout was founded in 1989. For many DC residents, it more than lives up to the tradition of its predecessor. Long lines that stretch well outside its doors attest to the restaurant's popularity.

DINING:

Levi's Restaurant

LOCATION: 10252 Lake Arbor Way, Mitchellville, MD
TELEPHONE: (301) 336-5000
PROPRIETOR: Young & Sue Kim
DRESS: Casual
MENU: NC Barbecue, Soul Food and Southern Cuisine
PRICE: Very Modest
HOURS: Tues – Sat 11:00 AM-10:00 PM
Sun Noon – 8:00 PM
URL: www.levisrestaurant.com

Comments: Sue Kim purchased this restaurant from Levi Durham, DC area restaurateur, in 1998. This is not her first venture in the soul food genre, having owned and operated a popular soul food restaurant for more than 20 years in Los Angeles. She has taken care to ensure that Levi Durham's recipes are followed in a manner that produces the same quality and flavorful results that Washington DC barbecue aficionados have come to know and love, adding her own nuances to make your dining experience just as memorable. Menu choices range from barbecue to soul food to southern cuisine. Some of their most request dishes include chopped barbecue, Cajun fried fish, barbecue ribs, smothered chicken, mac & cheese, rice & gravy and collard greens. The restaurant's atmosphere is both "down home" and tastefully appointed. Sue Kim is especially proud of the restaurant's commitment to her employees and the restaurant's role as a training environment for young, future entrepreneurs.

Manager Willie Martin, formerly with founder Levi Durham, has been with the restaurant from the beginning. Another member of the management team, Sherita Johnson, worked her way through Bowie State University here and gained invaluable experience in the restaurant business. She is an 11 year employee. The restaurant also does a vibrant catering business to local churches and schools. They also have catered for large government agencies such as the Departments of Commerce, Justice and Treasury. Levi's Restaurant is just 25 minutes east of the National Mall. It is a great choice for getting a "quick bite" during lunch or for dinner after a tour of Washington's fabulous monuments.

DINING:

Oohh's and Aahh's Soul Food Restaurant

LOCATION: 1005 U Street NW
TELEPHONE: (202) 667-7142
PROPRIETOR: India Wilson and Oji Abbot
DRESS: Casual
MENU: Soul Food
PRICE: Modest to Moderate
HOURS: Tues to Sat 12:00 PM – 10:00 PM; Sun 12:00 PM – 7:00 PM
URL: www.oohhsnaahhs.com

COMMENTS: Ooah's and Aahh's enjoys a popular following among Washingtonians. It is short on ambiance but it's a definite U Street neighborhood favorite. Their Mac & cheese usually garners rave reviews. The baked or fried chicken, crab cake sandwiches, collard greens and candied yams also are among their most requested dishes. The portions are very, very generous. Patience is key if you go during lunch hours because hungry customers sometimes are numerous, especially during week days.

DINING:

Saint's Paradise Cafeteria

LOCATION: 601A M Street NW (Corner of 6th & M)
TELEPHONE: (202) 789-2289
PROPRIETOR: United House of Prayer for All People
DRESS: Casual
MENU: Soul Food
PRICE: Modest
HOURS: Mon – Thur, 7:00 AM- 5:00 PM, Fri, 7:00 AM – 7:00 PM, Sat – Sun, 8:00 AM – 6:00 PM

COMMENTS: Saint's Paradise Cafeteria is an amazing soul food experience. Nestled in the basement of the United House of Prayer for All People, it has been serving up some of Washington DC's best "down home cooking" for over 70 years. Up until the mid-1980s, the cafeteria was a hidden gem known only to members of the Church. It then began serving the general public and quickly was adopted as a staple of the surrounding Mt Vernon community, now ranked among the best soul food restaurants in the Mid Atlantic area. The atmosphere brings back memories of "Church Suppers," the sort of quintessential soul food and religious experience known to many in the Southern United States. During my first visit, I stood in the cafeteria style serving line and could not help but marvel as patrons in front of me literally danced a jig in anticipation of the steaming hot fish and succulent turkey wings that were soon to be heaped onto Styrofoam plates. I tried the fried whiting, collard greens, mac & Cheese, and candied yams. After hoisting my take out and loading the brimming over Styrofoam plate into my car, I headed down Interstate 66 from DC to Northern Virginia. Within minutes, the aromas became so irresistible that I took the nearest exit, parked in a neighborhood cul-de-sac and feasted on the treats that Saints Paradise Cafeteria patrons have come to love. If you have a serious drive ahead of you, resisting the aromas of your take out without nibbling at the delights that await is a tall order. It's far better to sit down with your meal in this attractive, dining room style cafeteria and enjoy your soulful delights, fresh from the kitchen, piping hot and ready for immediate consumption. Saint's Paradise Cafeteria offers other menu treats such as smothered pork chops, fried chicken, meatloaf, cabbage and sweet potato pie. Theirs is a fellowship of cuisine and hospitality that you will want to place at the top of your list when looking for "down home cuisine" in our Nation's Capital.

Frederick Douglass Residence and Museum
located @ 320 A Street N.E.

Frederick Douglass Museum and Caring Hall
of Fame located @ 320 A Street N.E.

General Benjamin O. Davis Residence, U Street Corridor

Langston Hughes Residence, U Street Corridor

Historic Kappa Alpha Psi Fraternity House
(Kappa Kastle), 1708 S Street, NW

PREVIEW OF VOLUME II

THE NEXT EDITION OF AMERICAN

BLUES, JAZZ & SOUL FOOD ©

From White Sandy Beaches to Cotton Fields

Birmingham / Tuscaloosa, Alabama

Dining:

Dreamland Bar-B-Que

Location: 5535 15th Avenue, East Tuscaloosa
Telephone: 205-758-8135
Proprietor: John "Big Daddy" Bishop
Dress: Casual
Menu: Barbecue
Price: Modest
Hours: Mon – Thurs, 10:00AM – 9:00PM; Fri – Sat, 10:00AM – 10:00AM; Sun, 12:00PM – 9:00PM

Comments: John and Lillie Bishop founded Dreamland Bar-B-Que in 1958. Except for a few coats of fresh paint, the outside of the building has changed little since then. The sturdy red brick and pine structure is surrounded by wooden picket fences on a half-acre lot. Inside, the restaurant walls are alive with posters, photographs, and license plates. Some photos show the Bishop clan, while others profile visiting celebrities such as former Miami Dolphins football coach Don Shula, country singer Reba McEntire, and legendary Florida State football coach Bobby Bowden. Hundreds of bags of potato chips and Dreamland Bar-B-Que sauce (sold by the quart) line the shelf behind a long serving counter. An old wood-burning stove and piles of hickory, oak, and pecan wood stacked in front of the barbecue pit all add to the rustic ambiance. The dining room is expansive, but only seats about 60. Until 1980, this was just a popular neighborhood haunt. They served a full menu, sometimes including chitterlings. But the demand for pork barbecue grew so much that the restaurant had to start serving it exclusively to keep pace with the orders. When Lillie became ill, her daughter, Jeanette Bishop-Hall, was called in to run the business, and the restaurant has continued to soar. It has been featured on CNN, ESPN, NBC News with Tom Brokaw and The Oprah Winfrey Show, to name a few! *Atlanta* magazine, *Elle* magazine, and *The New York Times* have each done articles on it. The restaurant uses a cut of rib three and one-half down. The meat is barbecued precisely 45 minutes, marinated in its own juices and Dreamland's special sauce. This is one of the Southeast's true treasures. If you're traveling on 1-20 East/59 South, take exit 73 (McFarland Boulevard) and turn left onto McFarland. Go to the fourth signal and turn left onto Jug Factory Road. Follow the sign at the top of the hill.

Low Country
Charleston, SC to Savannah, GA

A road trip through the Low Country could begin in Charleston, travelling along 200 miles of coastland to the south, ending in Savannah, Georgia. Islands along your Low Country route could include Edisto, St. Helena, Hunting, Pinckney, Hilton Head, and Tybee. The city of Beaufort, SC is a convenient rest stop along the way.

When people speak of the Low country, one of the first things that come to mind is Low Country Cuisine. This southern fare is closely akin to Creole and Cajun Cuisine. The cultural influences are similar, European, Native American, African and the Caribbean; all coming together, a uniquely American cuisine evolving. The geographic landscape of the Low Country ideally provides a bounty of crab, shrimp, oysters, and wild game. With the introduction of livestock, sugar, white rice and okra from the "Old World," corn, peppers, sweet potatoes, tomatoes and white potatoes from Native Americans via Latin and South America, the perfect ingredients were in place for the emerging Low Country Cuisine.

Centuries before the arrival of immigrants from Europe, Native Americans were harvesting the wealth of the Low Country flora and fauna. Their food was derived from farming, fishing and hunting. Fresh water and salt water fishing provided clam, oysters, shrimp and crabs. Indian hunters brought home such game as deer, turkey, alligator, quail, duck and marsh hens. They also grew corn, squash and various beans (lima, snap, green, kidney, navy, etc.). The gifts of tomatoes, potatoes, peppers and sweet potatoes migrated to North America thanks to the Indians of South America and Latin America. Christopher Columbus brought other food staples to the "New World," obtained or discovered by way of ancient trade routes, such as bananas, coffee, rice, sugar cane, salt, wheat and livestock that included cattle, goats, horses, and chickens during the 15th century.

Some of these staples that were brought to the "New World" directly contributed to and set into motion the industry of slavery. The emergence of South Carolina and Georgia's Low Country as a fertile region for growing rice, coveted by the rest of the world, fueled demand for the importation of African Slaves. The global demand for rice directly correlated to the desire for slave labor to plant, cultivate and harvest rice. The Port of Charleston became one of the largest points of embarkation for African Slaves, primarily from West Africa by way of the Caribbean. African slaves also were desired because of their familiarity with rice cultivation. Many were farmers from the West African coastal areas of Sierra Leone, Ghana, Ivory Coast, Togo and Benin, where rice farming predominated.

All of these factors contributed to the merger of West African, Caribbean, European and Native American culture. Low Country Cuisine evolved as a unique culinary art form. A popular Low Country dish is Frogmore Stew (AKA Lowcountry Boil), a dish consisting of shrimp, corn on the cobb, and spicy sausage, all boiled together in one pot and served on a plate. One of the national dishes of Gambia is called the "Benechin" or "One pot", where fish, meat, vegetables and spices are cooked in one pot as a stew. Another Low Country favorite is "Hoppin John," a flavorful dish of rice cooked with black-eyed peas. Rice, black-eyed peas and okra were essential elements of meals consumed in many areas of West Africa long before the America's were colonized.

In summary, Low Country Cuisine is a unique culinary experience that blends "Old World" with the "New World." The culinary traditions of ancient civilizations from the Aztec and Incas with their peppers, tomatoes, potatoes and the like- to ancient China with rice- to Ancient Egypt with okra- to India with processed sugar- to Africa with its human treasures, long suffering as slaves- to the bounty of the low country estuaries, marshes and Atlantic coast- and to the native Americans who were, at first, welcoming hosts to the new arrivals.

Dining:

Alluette's Cafe

80 A Reid Street
Charleston, SC
843-577-6926
Propprietor: Alluette Jones-Smalls
Dress: Casual/Classy
Menu: Soul Food, Vegan, Gullah & Gheechi Tradition
Price: Modest
Hours: Mon – Wed: 11:00 AM-7:00 PM, Thur - Sat: 11 AM – 9:00 PM
URL: www.alluettes.com

Comments: Alluette Jones-Smalls serves up "Gheechi Girl Turkey Burgher," Fried or Grilled Shrimp, Whiting, Croaker, Flounder, & Red Snapper according to market availability, and "Sought after Salad" featuring Hormone- and Antibiotic-free Chicken Breast, prepared with a blend of Gheechi Girl herbs and spices, served on a bed of fresh organic seasonal greens. This restaurateur hangs her hat on the mantle of "holistic soul food." Foodies throughout the country have taken notice. Oprah.com, Southern Living, Travel & Leisure, O Magazine, Chow Hound and the local City Paper are among the many magazine, news and social media outlets that have given favorable reviews.

Bertha's Kitchen

2332 Meeting Street RD
Charleston, SC
843-554-6519
Proprietor: The Grant Sisters (Julia, Linda and Sharon)
Dress: Casual/Classy
Menu: Soul Food, Gullah Tradition
Price: Very Modest
Hours: Mon – Fri: 11:00 AM-7:00 PM

Comments: Bertha's Kitchen was founded by the late Albertha Grant. This tiny, roadside eatery has been a North Charleston mainstay for over 30 years. Locals rave about their fried fish, fried chicken, pork chops, Lima beans, rice n gravy, and okra stew. They were closed the Friday after thanksgiving during my last vist. Can't wait to get there again and try their stew beef, lima beans over rice, yams and corn bread.

Dave's Carry-Out

42 Morris ST, Suite C
Charleston, SC
Telephone: 843-577-7943
Proprietor: Terry McCray
Dress: Casual/Classy
Menu: Seafood, Low Country Tradition
Price: Very Modest
Hours: Tues – Fri: Lunch and Supper
Specialties: Fried Seafood

Comments: This is the "go to place" for local fish lovers. Whether you try their fried fish sandwich or opt for the fried shrimp atop a bed of red rice and collards, you're sure to see why this "hole in the wall" gets rave reviews.

Miss Charlotte's Gullah Cuisine

1717 N Hwy 17
Mount Pleasant, SC 29464-3314
(843) 881-9076
Proprietor: Charlotte Jenkins
Dress: Casual/Classy
Menu: Seafood, Lowcountry Tradition
Price: Very Modest
Hours: Tues – Fri: Lunch and Supper
http://gullahcuisine.net

Comments: Miss Charlotte's Gullah Cuisine restaurant is a throwback to days long gone. Her menu can be traced back to the early 1700's, when West African families bought their knowledge and expertise in the art of growing rice to the coastal plains of South Carolina. They inhabited South Carolina's coastal islands, areas that were inhospitable to Europeans but well suited for them due to their acquired immunities to Malaria. Because of their isolation, much of their culture remained intact ; their language (Gullah), cuisine (West African influenced) and customs (Gambia, Ghana, Ivory Coast, Senegal et al). Accordingly, Gullah Cuisine honors the Gullah Culture of their ancestors, providing a menu that is much influenced by the flavorful dishes of West African, Native America and Europe.

Their Gullah Rice is a must have, blending white rice, green peppers & Onions, shrimp, chicken, sausage, and vegetables into "a meal in itself" dish that is sure to please. Other items from the menu include Low Country Crab Cakes, Okra Gumbo, Seafood Gumbo and Shrimp with Hominy. In addition an afternoon helping of Gullah Rice, I tried their candied yams, corn bread muffins and sweet tea. It truly was a great meal that did me well for the rest of the day. The staff of Gullah Cuisine is very attentive, radiating southern hospitality at its finest and always eager to share their knowledge of Gullah Culture.

Martha Lou's Kitchen

1068 Morrison Drive
Charleston, SC
Telephone: 843-577-9583
http://marthalouskitchen.com/
Proprietor: Martha Lou Gadsden
Dress: Casual/Classy
Menu: Soul Food, Gullah Tradition
Price: Modest
Hours: Mon – Fri: Breakfast and Lunch

Comments: Martha Lou's Kitchen is landmark restaurant that was founded in 1983. Specialties include Collard greens, lima beans, and cornbread with pork chops or beef stew, fish or fried chicken; with choice of beverage (ask for the sweet tea).

Scott's Bar-B-Que

2734 Hemingway Hwy.
Hwy. 261 & Brunson Cross Road
Hemingway, SC 29554
843-558-0134
URL: www.thescottsbbq.com

Comments: Ella and Roosevelt "Rosie" Scott founded this landmark establishment in 1972. The predecessor of Scott's Bar-B-Que originally was a small country store, garage and pool hall. The initial products sold were perishables, canned goods, auto repair services and the like. A couple of hogs were smoked on the weekends and shared with guests, family and friends. The whole hog quickly became the staple of choice. As a result, the old general store and garage morphed into Hemingway South Carolina's "Hidden Gem;" where whole hogs are smoked to perfection. A regional and nationwide following continues to gain momentum. A host of media outlets such as the New York Times, Washington Post, Charlotte Observer, CBS News, NBC News and Southern Living Magazine have provided glowing reviews. Southern Foodways Alliance published a documentary on Scott's Bar-B-Cue in 2012. Rodney Scott, son of Rosie and Ella, is one 18 nationally renowned Pit Masters invited to the Big Apple Barbecue festival in New York's Madison Square Park annually. The national acclaim of Scott's Bar-B-Q continues to soar. Pit Master Scott was one of 10 entrepreneurs in the country to receive the American Treasures Award for 2012.

Walking up to the restaurant, one has the feeling of being transported back in time. Rodney Scott and several relatives saunter back and forth between a huge fire barrel and hand-made pits at the rear of the property. Rodney shovels red hot coals of oak or hickory, sometimes pecan wood, from fire barrel to pit. The aromas of barbecue and peppery-vinegary sauce billow and dance in the smoke filled air. Baskets of sweet potatoes are strewn about the front porch. Locals also find the front porch a cozy gathering place, communing on wooden benches, Church Pews in their former life. A half dozen cars vie for space on the restaurant's gravel lot, their license plates suggesting long time patrons and barbecue pilgrims all are gathered here, from nearby locales in the Pee Dee Region to faraway places across the United States.

Houston, Texas

JAZZ/BLUES/REGGAE:

Etta's Lounge and Restaurant

Location: 5120 Scott Street
Telephone: 713-528-2611
Clientele: Young/Mature Adult
Format: Blues
Calendar: Live Entertainment Sunday
Cover/Minimum: Yes/No
Dress: Casual/Classy

Comments: Whenever I venture into one of these old-style blues clubs, I wonder how long places like Etta's will continue to dot the nation's landscape. Forever, I hope. But when you talk to the staff at Etta's, they lament that they're not as active as they once were, having scaled down from offering live entertainment all weekend to just on Sunday evenings. "The economy is the culprit," they are quick to point out. Nevertheless, Etta's continues to be an important club in Houston that one evening each week. On Sundays, the venerable sax man Grady Gaines descends on Etta's with his Upsetters Band and transforms the place. The club is bare on the outside, not even yielding its name to the casual observer. Inside, it's also bare, but spacious and attractive in a simple way. Against this backdrop, Gaines and the Upsetters hold court for an appreciative audience comprised of Houstonians from throughout the city. Playing a range of music from Texas blues to R&B, the band sizzles on tunes by artists such as Muddy Waters, Joe Tex, Al Green, and Marvin Gaye.

Houston, Texas

Dining:

This Is It

Location: 207 W. Gray Street
Telephone: 713-523-5319
Proprietor: Craig Joseph
Dress: Casual/Classy
Menu: Soul Food
Price: Very Modest
Hours: Mon – Sat 11:00AM – 8:00PM; Sun 11:00 AM – 6:00 PM
URL: www.thisisithouston.com

Comments: The late Frank and Mattie Jones founded This Is It in 1959. Before that, he had a barbecue restaurant in Los Angeles during the 1930s. He and his wife Mattie started out in Houston as a mom-and-pop business, operating for 24 years out of their home at 1003 Andrews Street, in the heart of the Fourth Ward. In response to their enormous popularity, they moved to their current location and built the restaurant from the ground up. Jones retired in 1992, turning This Is it over to his grandson Craig Joseph. Through the years, the restaurant has evolved into Houston's most popular soul-food eatery. It is short on frills, but spacious and attractive. A pair of gold records above the doorway commemorates the hits "Mr. Scarface Is Back" and "Till Death do Us Part". Both were presented to the restaurant by the rap group the Geto Boys, also products of Houston's Fourth Ward. A celebrity wall depicts past customers such as BB King, Johnnie Taylor, and Bobby Womack. According to Joseph, the Reverend Jesse Jackson is also a frequent visitor. In fact, the last time he came, he spent most of the evening waiting on tables and chatting with the guests. This is a place to bring your friends and family, settle into a booth or pull a few tables together, and enjoy a great meal. I made myself right at home and proceeded to dispatch a generous portion of cabbage, pinto beans, and rice and gravy garnished with smothered pork chops. A glass of ice cold lemonade was just the right complement for the delicious meal. Folks have been repeating this scenario at This Is It for more than three decades. The most popular entrees are the ox tails and chitterlings. Other menu items include meatloaf, pepper steak, turkey wings, lima beans, and candied yams. Put this eatery at the top of your list when visiting the city.

Jackson, Mississippi

JAZZ/BLUES/REGGAE:

Hal & Mal's Restaurant & Oyster Bar

Location: 200 S. Commerce Street
Telephone: 601-948-0888
Clientele: Young/Mature Adult
Format: Blues/Rock and Roll
Calendar: Live Entertainment Varies
Cover/Minimum: Yes/No
Dress: Casual/Classy
URL: www.halandmals.com

Comments: Hal and Mal's Restaurant & Oyster Bar is located in an old warehouse that once served as one of Jackson's busiest freight depots. In 1986, Malcolm White, his wife Vivian, and his brother Harold leased the entire complex and converted it into Jackson's premier entertainment showcase. Over the years, the club has featured blues stars such as Bobby "Blue" Bland, Otis Clay, the late Albert King, and BB King. The Tangents, a blues and R&B group from the Delta, Patrice Moncell, and Miss Molly and the Whips are some of their most popular local acts. The restaurant occupies three rooms in the front of the complex. Each is accented in sea green, and the main dining room displays numerous early transistor radios. Adjacent to the restaurant, but accessible through another entrance, is a small entertainment venue. The carpeted room lined with vinyl booths features a large stage. Beyond this room is yet another entertainment area, simply called the "Big Room." This room spanning almost the entire length of the complex has a hardwood floor and a large concert stage. It holds at least 700, while the smaller room accommodates about 200. A patio in the back, enclosed by a high, red brick wall, provides yet another entertainment option. Besides great music in an intimate setting, an evening at Hal and Mal's also offers a dining experience that stands on its own merits. The best red beans and rice this side of New Orleans, fried or grilled catfish, and seafood platters are but a few of the delights. The desserts include mouth-watering chocolate silk pies and praline ice cream. The restaurant, which seats 90, is open for lunch and dinner Monday through Friday from 11:00 AM and for dinner on Saturday from 5:00 PM. Hal and Mal's have been featured in *Connoisseur*, *Esquire*, the *Mississippi Business Journal*, and the local daily, the *Clarion Ledger*. Stop by, and you will understand why.

Jackson, Mississippi

DINING:

Bully's Restaurant

Location: 3118 Livingstone Road
Telephone: 601-362-0484
Proprietor: W. G. Bully
Dress: Casual/Classy
Menu: Soul Food
Price: Very Modest
Hours: Mon – Thurs 11:00 AM – 6:00 PM; Fri – Sat 11:00 AM – 8:00 PM

Comments: Ask most Jackson residents where you can find the best soul-food fare in the city and the answer, more often than not, is Bully's Restaurant – they love the down-home taste of the food and the generous helpings. An entree such as smothered roast beef comes piled high with tender meat and three succulent vegetables. You also get dessert and two cornbread muffins! I tried the roast beef with a side order of mixed greens, butter beans, rice and gravy, and corn bread. By the time I had eaten half of it, I realized that I'd better taste the peach cobbler before I could eat no more. The meal rates among the ten best I've tried since I started work on this book. The restaurant is a small, attractive eatery located less than ten minutes from downtown Jackson. Sit-down diners will find the space a bit cramped; the seating accommodates only about 25. A smaller room at the entrance is where most patrons queue up, because take-out is the order of the day here. Longtime residents of Jackson usually call ahead to order their favorite dishes. It's also best to come early in the day because the most popular dishes sell out quickly. Beef tips and rice, boiled neck bones, and smothered pork chops are the items that normally go fastest. Other entrees include catfish fillers, ham hocks, pan-fried trout, and oxtail. Vegetable selections include fried corn, cabbage, and yams along with homemade desserts such as lemon icebox pie and cheesecake. W. G. Bully founded the restaurant in 1981. His wife Robbie, son Tyrone, and daughter-in-law Grete all lend a hand in the day-to-day operation of the restaurant. Tyrone Bully cites the quality of the food and the dedicated work ethic of each family member as keys to the success of the restaurant. Featured by the *Clarion Ledger* as the city's top soul-food restaurant, Bully's also provides catering services, primarily for family reunions and weddings.

Little Rock, Arkansas

JAZZ/BLUES/REGGAE:

Juanita's Mexican Cafe & Bar

Location: 1300 Main Street
Telephone: 501-372-1228
Clientele: Young/Mature Adult
Format: Blues/Reggae/Rock
Calendar: Live Entertainment Wed - Sat
Cover/Minimum: Yes/No
Dress: Casual/Classy
URL: www.juanitas.com

Comments: Juanita's Mexican Cafe & Bar has long been considered one of Little Rock's top entertainment showcases. First-time visitors will be swept away immediately by the club's character and charm. The first thing that greets customers upon entering is a bin filled with Texas onions, garlic cloves, jalapeno peppers, and lemons. Red booths line one side of the dining room. A passageway leads to the bar and entertainment room on the left. A large stage sits in the corner, canted so that it faces the entire room. Wooden rails divide the room into thirds: one area with cocktail tables along the bar, a sunken area in the center with another set of tables, and a third area against the far wall with both tables and a dance floor. Graffiti covers the far wall. An outdoor patio with long wooden tables and umbrellas provides a comfortable interlude between sessions by the band. During my first visit, I caught a rousing performance by RAS recording stars the Mystic Revealers. Lead singer Billy Mystic and DJ Soljah captivated the audience with songs from their debut album Young Revolutionaries. The music at Jaunita's ranges from jazz to reggae to rock & roll. Among the acts that have appeared here are reggae stars Sister Carol, Mikey Dread, and Roots Radies; blues stars Major Handy, Kenny Neal, Duke Robillard, Koko Taylor, and the Kinsey Report; and jazz standouts Hank Crawford and Jimmy McGriff. The club's reggae line-up garnered them recognition as the "Best Reggae Night Club of 1991" by the Mid-American Music Awards. Juanita's consistently has been acknowledged as the best

Mexican restaurant in central Arkansas by the *Arkansas Times Magazine*. The menu offers at intriguing array of delights from south of the border, including mesquite-grilled fish and the Mexican dinner de San Antonio. And, of course, there are the margaritas! Open daily for lunch and dinner, this is one you won't want to pass up.

Little Rock, Arkansas

Dining:

Lindsey's Hospitality House

Location: 207 E. 15th Street (North Little Rock, Ark)
Telephone: 501-374-5707
Proprietor: Donnie Lindsey
Dress: Casual/Classy
Menu: Barbecue/Southern
Price: Very Modest
Hours: Mon – Fri 11:00 AM – 6:00 PM
URL: www.lindseysbbqnmore.com

Comments: Lindsey's Hospitality House is both a restaurant and a full-service banquet facility. A small room at the front of the restaurant includes a long display case holding an assortment of delights such as pecan, lemon meringue, and sweet-potato pie. The dining room is attractively decorated in light blue with long wall mirrors and African American folk art throughout. An archway at the rear of the dining room leads to an elegant banquet room in soft pastels, with a mix of cafe and banquet-shaped dining tables and glass chandelier. The rooms seat 70 and 200, respectively. Bishop Lindsey founded Little Rock's fabled Lindsey's Bar-B-Que in 1956, then took a break from the restaurant business for almost two decades. He opened this complex in 1989. The building also includes a religious bookstore operated by his wife Irma and a beauty salon operated by his daughter Donna. Another daughter, DeJuana, and son Donnie Jr. co-managed the restaurant from the beginning; however, son Donnie Jr. now serves as owner and operator. The most-requested items on the menu are beef short ribs, smothered chicken, fresh mixed greens, candied yams, and fried, hot-water cornbread. The cornbread is light but firm, similar in texture and taste to cake. During hunting season, the restaurant also does a thriving business preparing game that customers bring in from the field. They have a long list of patrons who come by to have their venison smoked, for example. The restaurant's banquet room is a local favorite for family and class reunions, wedding receptions, and special events such as the National Conference of Black Ministers hosted by President Bill Clinton's 1992 campaign staff. The restaurant also caters for a wide range of civic and public organizations, ranging from the school system to state and municipal arms of government. Lindsey's Hospitality House is yet another of little Rock's outstanding soul food restaurants, each of which rates among the best in the Southeast.

Miami, Florida

Jazz/Blues/Reggae

Tobacco Road

Location: 626 S. Miami Avenue
Telephone: 305-374-1198
Clientele: Young/Mature Adult
Format: Jazz/Blues
Calendar: Live Entertainment Nightly
Cover/Minimum: Yes/No
Dress: Casual/Classy
URL: www.tobacco-road.com

Comments: Tobacco Road is one of the oldest blues clubs in the Southeast. Established in 1912, the club also boasts the oldest liquor license in Miami, Number 001. In its early years, it served as a speakeasy. Ask any bartender or waitress, and he or she will gleefully tell you about the secret room upstairs where contraband alcohol was hidden during Prohibition. In 1982, Patrick Gleber and Kevin Rusk purchased the club and converted it to a Mecca for blues artists. When you walk through the door, glance to the left, and view photographs of previous artists that depict virtually a history of blues in the United States. Legendary musicians such as Clarence "Gatemouth" Brown, the late Albert Collins, Johnny Copeland, John Lee Hooker, BB King, and Charlie Musselwhite have all performed here. One display includes a photo and plaque in memory of longtime employee Willie "Doc Feelgood" Bell. The first-floor bar is a narrow room with booths and a hardwood-topped bar spanning two-thirds of the room, all converging on a small passageway towards the rear and adjacent stage. Here is where local blues acts most often perform, as do the opening acts for major shows held upstairs. Getting a view of the band from many areas of the room can be a challenge. This area and the patio accommodate about 75 patrons. Upstairs is the Diamond Teeth Mary Cabaret, named in memory of blues and gospel singer Mary Smith McCain. The cabaret has the feel and look of a traditional blues room: red walls, painted black floors, and tables decked with red tablecloths. The room has about 60 seats, all providing a good view of the stage. By day, Tobacco Road is a neighborhood bar. At night, local blues favorite Iko Iko, the house band since 1982, packs them in. After the opening acts perform downstairs, the crowd typically makes a beeline for seats upstairs, so you should plan your strategy accordingly!

Mississippi Delta

JAZZ/BLUES/REGGAE:

Ground Zero Blues Club

Location: 0 Blues Alley Ln, Clarksdale, MS
Telephone: 662-621-9009
Clientele: Young/Mature Adult
Format: Blues
Calendar: Live Entertainment Weds - Sat
Cover/Minimum:
Dress: Casual / Classy
www.groundzerobluesclub.com

Comments: The Ground Zero Blues Club is the brainchild of owners Morgan Freeman, Jr., award winning actor, director and narrator; local attorney and businessman, Bill Luckett; and Clarksdale native and Memphis entertainment executive, Howard Stovall. Their vision of a local venue for live performance blues where blues had its beginnings was well worth the risk. It has become one of the treasures of Clarksdale. The grand opening of the Ground Zero Blues Club on May 27, 2001 was met with great anticipation throughout the Delta and, of course, Clarksburg, MS. The club opened a week earlier and patrons were numerous and excited. The grand opening did not disappoint. Acclaimed actress Ashley Judd and her sister, country music star Wynonna Judd, arrived to help celebrate. Clarksdale residents were almost giddy with delight. Blues legend Pinetop Perkins, the featured artist, was a great choice for the grand opening honors. Delta born, he represents one of the last great bridges to the birth of the blues, churning out Delta Blues on guitar, then piano for over three quarters of a century. Since its opening, the Ground Zero blues club has been featured in numerous local, national and international publications. Their primary focus is the exhibition of established and promising local Delta Blues artists; however, national acts continue to make their way here. A live DVD recording entitled "Down To The Crossroads – Volume 1" featuring George Thorogood and the Destroyers with legendary blues man Eddie Shaw was the first of a series hosted by Morgan Freeman and filmed at the club. The ambiance is authentically delta, from the uneven plank floors to the portraits of Delta Blues legends displayed throughout. Since its founding, Ground Zero Blues Club has received international acclaim. Its merits have been lauded on television and in print publications by media as diverse as National Geographic Traveler, Esquire Japan, Southern Living, USA Today, CBS 60 Minutes and the Food Network. Morgan Freeman lives in nearby Charleston, MS. You may catch a glimpse of him here or you can saunter over to his elegant Madidi Restaurant located just two blocks away.

Nashville, Tennessee

Dining:

Swett's Restaurant

Location: 2725 Clifton Avenue
Telephone: 615-329-4418
Proprietor: The Swett Family
Dress: Casual/Classy
Menu: Soul Food/Southern
Price: Very Modest
Hours: Daily 11:00 AM – 9:00 PM
URL: www.swettsrestaurant.com

Comments: Swett's is Nashville's largest and most popular soul-food restaurant. The restaurant sits at the far end of the parking lot on the corner of Clifton and 28th. The main dining room, on the right as you enter, is swathed in red brick and soft lavender. The outer portion of the dining room is a cozy patio encased in glass. The opposite side of the building consists of a dining room with similar décor; this is most often used when the main room overflows or for private parties. The entire facility seats almost 200. A long serving line, partially concealed from view in the main dining room, holds tray of piping-hot dishes such as meatloaf, fried chicken, smothered pork chops, fried catfish, candied yams, steamed cabbage, turnip greens and hoe cakes. Their beef tips, diced beef in a mushroom gravy, are the most requested entree. Susie and Walter Swett founded the restaurant in 1954. Starting out in a little white building on the corner of their current location, it was a modest affair that sold beer and sandwiches. Shortly after opening, Susie Swett decided to prepare a full meal that included chitterlings, turnips, green beans, and yams just to see how the items would sell. It was an instant success. By the early 1960s, the Swetts weren't selling much beer, but they were selling a lot of soul food. In 1972, they remodeled the restaurant and featured the current cafeteria style. Walter Swett retired in 1979, selling the restaurant to sons David Sr. and Morris. In 1988, they built a larger, more modern restaurant that was destroyed by fire within 30 days of its completion. They held the grand reopening of the current facility in April 1989. A third generation of Swetts, David Jr. and Patrick, work at the restaurant. Another son, Alberto, and daughter Nikki also have helped. This is a family affair celebrating over 50 years in the business. Be sure to stop in and enjoy some down-home cooking when you're visiting Nashville.

North Carolina Triangle, Chapel Hill:

DINING:

Mama Dip's

Location: 408 W. Rosemary Street
Telephone: 919-942-5837
Proprietor: Mildred "Dip" Council
Menu: Southern
Dress: Casual/Classy
Price: Very Modest
Hours: Mon – Fri 8:00 AM – 3:00 PM, 4:00 PM – 10:00 PM; Sat 8:00 AM – 10:00 PM; Sun 8:00 AM – 9:00 PM
URL: www.mamadips.com

Comments: Dip's is one of the most attractive soul-food places in the Triangle. The restaurant is all earth tones, old brick and mortar, and cedar paneling. On the countertop, a wicker display case is lined with jars of Mama Dip's Poppy Seed Dressing and Mama Dip's Bar-B-Que Sauce. Five sets of booths, all hardwood and black leather, line the far wall of the main dining room on the right. The picture windows look out onto a stand of trees, giving the illusion of dining at grandma's house and, afterwards, sitting out on the veranda. According to Mama Dip's granddaughter Cissy, the barbecue ribs and the lightly battered fried chicken are the most requested entrees.

The Country Breakfast includes staples such as salmon cake, chicken and gravy, country ham, and eggs, all served with a choice of grits or hash browns and piping hot biscuits or toast. Additional entrees include combination plates with barbecue chicken and ribs, chopped barbecue with chicken, and Brunswick stew and barbecue chicken and dumplings. A tantalizing array of desserts such as pecan, apple, and sweet potato pies; German chocolate, lemon and orange pound, and coconut cakes; and peach and apple cobblers also are too good to pass up. Mildred Council has been in this location almost 18 years. She originally started with a small restaurant. Over the years, its popularity grew, and she purchased the adjacent property, had one wall knocked out, and created the country-inn ambiance the restaurant enjoys today. It seats about 80 diners. Council's barbecue sauce is a tomato-based recipe that dates back to 1957. Daughters Elaine and Spring and son Joe are each actively involved in the restaurant. So is a third generation, represented by grandchildren Cissy, Sherry, and Tonya. Stop by and experience down-home ambiance, Southern hospitality, and outstanding Southern cuisine.

Orlando, Florida

Dining:

Johnson's Diner

Location: 595 W. Church St
Telephone: 407-841-0717
Proprietor: The Johnson Family
Dress: Casual
Menu: Soul Food
Price: Very Modest
Hours: Mon – Weds 7:00 AM – 4:00 PM; Thurs 7:00 AM – 7:00PM; Fri & Sat 7:00 AM – 8:00 PM; Sun 12:00 PN – 4:00 PM
www.johnsonsdiner.com

Comments: Orlando is a fun filled destination that family members dream about, especially as the end of the school year approaches and visions of Disney capture the imaginations of school children. Once you made that trip to Disney and the family is immersed in fanciful attractions too numerous to mention, consider taking a moment to travel across town and experience an Orlando soul food attraction. Johnson's Diner is Orlando's most iconic. The Diner was founded in 1963 by Lillie Johnson, located in the city's historic Paramore neighborhood. The restaurant prospered and grew a wide customer base while located at its modest digs on the corner of Robinson Street and Paramore Avenue for over two decades. Seating was limited and carryout was the order of the day. Nevertheless, Johnson's Diner managed to attract clientele from across Orlando, the state and nationwide. Luminaries who have dropped represent wide swaths of the political and entertainment spectrum: Congressman Alcee Hastings, NBA star Shaquille O'Neal, Actor Wesley Snipes and Master P, to name a few. With the help of a grant from Orlando's Destination Activity Catalyst Program, the restaurant relocated to its current location in 2006. Their menu items that made them renowned have not changed; however, available dishes are rotated daily; depending on when you visit, delightful choices such as breakfast fish and grits with hotcakes, cornmeal crusted fried fish, smothered chicken, chitterlings, mustard or collard greens are among their favorite offerings. Johnson's Diner is a Third Generation landmark restaurant. On 25 February, 2010, the restaurant was given The Orlando Sentinel's "Critic's Choice Award," best restaurant in Central Florida in the category of African / Soul / Caribbean. In the words of the Orlando Sentinel Food Editor, Heather McPherson, "Go for the fried chicken and leave room for sweet potato pie."

Hall of Memories

The Hall of Memories is dedicated to outstanding soul food restaurants and blues or jazz venues whose doors have closed. Each venue profiled here was widely recognized for excellence in its respective community. America's fabled "Chittlin Circuit," a safe harbor of theaters and supper clubs where entertainers of color performed from the late 1800s to the late 1960s, provided opportunities to experience the artistry and magic of the early Gospel, Blues, Jazz, and R&B greats. Many of these establishments have receded from memory, recalled only by old timers and cultural historians. Harlem's Cotton Club, the Howard Theatre in Washington D.C., the Royal Peacock Club in Atlanta and the Dreamland Ballroom of Little Rock were among the many establishments where you could hear and see legendary artists such as Bobby "Blue" Bland, Billie Holiday, Duke Ellington, Ella Fitzgerald, Albert King, and many, many more.

While attending Morehouse College in 1968, I would often go to Alex's Barbecue on West Hunter Street (now Martin Luther King, Jr. Boulevard) or Paschal's Restaurant just down the street, or the Auburn Avenue Grill; taking a break from school cafeteria fare, devouring their delicious barbecue and soul food. While many institutions like these have closed, they still retain substantial economic value. Their excellence and goodwill are waiting to be recalled, rejoining their respective communities as much-needed employers and economic drivers.

Thanks to the vision of a few entrepreneurs and city planners, some of these venues have been reborn. Washington DC's Lincoln Theatre has been beautifully restored and has returned to prominence as one of the city's treasures. On Sept. 2nd, 2010, the city broke ground on a restoration project that signals the return of the historic Howard Theatre, a landmark entertainment venue that dates back to 1910. The city of Richmond, VA, also has launched a campaign to restore yet another historic venue, the Hippodrome

Theatre. These outstanding renovation projects have been embraced by music aficionados from near and far, providing a model for others to follow.

Note: Restaurants and music venues close for reasons that are many and varied. An epilogue is included with some of the entries listed here when additional information is available to the author.

Hall of Memories: ATLANTA, GA

JAZZ/BLUES/REGGAE:

JUST JAZZ

Location: 595 Piedmont Rd, NE
Telephone: (404) 897-1555
Clientele: Young/Mature Adult
Format: Jazz
Calendar: Live Entertainment Nightly
Cover/Minimum: Yes/No
Dress: Classy
Status: **Closed**

Comments: Just Jazz developed quite a following after it appeared on Atlanta's jazz scene in 1991. Proprietor J. O. Wyatt, a former Fulton County commissioner, felt that if Atlanta was truly to emerge as an international destination, the city needed a top-flight jazz club that regularly featured some of America's touring jazz legends. The city's response to Just Jazz exceeded even his expectations. A noticeably international clientele thronged to the club's doors. What was all the fuss about? The answer, simply, was outstanding jazz. If you came in for a performance by the house band, what you got was the fabulous Johnny O'Neal Trio. O'Neal, formerly of the Jazz Messengers, was accompanied by Little Jimmy Scott's nephew, Kermit Walker, on drums, and Berkeley School of Music graduate Ramon Pooser on bass. On other evenings, you could expect touring performers such as Kenny Burrel, George Duke, Milt Jackson, and Cassandra Wilson. Celebrated artists frequently dropped by and, unannounced, sat in with the band. Jazz pianist Joe Sample, Stevie Wonder and the siren of blues and jazz, Nancy Wilson, all did. The theme was musical throughout, from the timbal drum that served as a ticket holder at the door to the grand piano-shaped bar inside. The décor was sleek black and white. The club seated about 200, but could expand to 300 when they opened their private party room to accommodate the largest shows. Just Jazz's success did not go unnoticed. It was proclaimed best jazz club in the city by Atlanta Magazine for 1992 and 1993. A reader's poll in the underground newspaper Creative Loafing voted it best in 1993 as well. An equally impressive accolade came from the July 1993 issue of Details magazine, where the club was cited among the "top 300 nights out from Halifax to Honolulu."

JAZZ/BLUES/REGGAE:

LA CAROUSEL

Location: 830 Martin Luther King, Jr., Blvd
Telephone: (404) 577-3150
Clientele: Mature Adult
Format: Jazz
Calendar: Live Entertainment Fri – Sat
Cover/Minimum: No/Yes (1 drink)
Dress: Classy
Status: **Closed**

Comments: La Carousel, located in the historic Paschal's Hotel, was a beautiful testament to the vision of the hotel's founders, James and Robert Paschal. As you entered from the restaurant, a platform encased in glass allowed you to view the entire club. After taking a seat on one of the circular bar's comfortable stools, partially covered with soft white leather, a feeling of something intangible permeated the air. Perhaps it was an aura of power, of momentous action lying at the edge of something yet unspoken. After all, this was a room where Atlantans came to discuss matters of import for decades. From conversations that stirred around the bar, you would hear men and women waxing poetic on subjects ranging from local campaign plans to urban renewal projects. Overhead was a colorful canopy of the kind you would find on a merry-go-round. Two antique wooden carousel horses pranced in one corner. Murals depicted pensive circus clowns. Many jazz and R&B legends played here. Jazz pianist Ramsey Lewis performed for the club's grand opening in 1959, and Ray Charles, Lou Rawls, and Count Basie were among the long list of renowned entertainers who followed. During the late 1980s, the club's focus shifted from national acts, preferring instead to showcase local jazz artists. The late Herman Mitchell and his Trio were among the last to headline in what was one of the coziest and most attractive jazz rooms in town.

Epilogue: La Carousel was included in the sale of Paschal's Hotel and Restaurant to Clark-Atlanta University in 2002.

DINING:

ALECK'S BARBECUE HEAVEN

LOCATION: 783 Martin Luther King, Jr. Blvd
TELEPHONE: (404) 525-2062
PROPRIETOR: Pamela Alexander
DRESS: Casual
MENU: Barbecue/Soul Food
PRICE: Modest
Status: **Closed**

Comments: Ernest Alexander built this rib house in the early 1950s, and it became one of the great Southern barbecue restaurants in the South. Alexander's daughter Pamela maintained the family tradition well. After winning a seat on Atlanta's City Council, she had lots of help keeping the restaurant going. You would often find a third generation of Alexanders tending the grill. The service was excellent, the ribs and veggies superb, and the flavors and aromas reminded me of summertime family reunions. I often ate here when I was a student in the 1960s and I will always remember this restaurant as one of my favorites.

DINING:

AUBURN AVENUE RIB SHACK

Location: 302 Auburn Ave, NE
Telephone: (404) 523-8315
Proprietor: Dorothy Clements
Dress: Casual
Menu: Barbecue/Soul Food
Price: Modest
Status: **Closed**

Comments: This historic rib house was founded by Allen J. and Mary C. Taylor in 1962. Allen Taylor opened his first restaurant, a popular barbecue shop on Bell Street, in the early 1950s. According to his daughter Dorothy Clements, this experience, which was a business partnership, cemented his love affair with the restaurant business. Taylor operated several other small sandwich shops in Atlanta's West End during the late 1950s and early 1960s, and when he got the chance to acquire a property on Atlanta's still-booming Auburn Avenue in 1962, he leapt at it. That was a time when, as Clements recalled, you could walk down Auburn Avenue on Sundays and see African Americans dressed to the hilt. A life-long member of the historic Ebenezer Baptist Church, she would spend Sunday mornings in church and then ask permission to watch the elaborate parades put on by the Elks and Price Hall Masons. The Reverend William Holmes Borders and the Reverend Martin Luther King, Sr. would patrol the avenue, tending to the faithful. King Sr.'s entire family would stop by the restaurant for barbecue. Clements took over the restaurant in 1982, fulfilling a promise she made to her late father. Her mother, Mary Taylor, made the secret, tomato-based barbecue sauce from scratch. This establishment still occupies a special place in the hearts and memories of many long time Atlanta citizens. The succulent barbecue ribs were the most requested dish on the menu. Many also favored the collard greens and macaroni & cheese. The restaurant was tiny by any standard, with seating for 12, so most patrons would stop by for take-out orders. The Auburn Avenue Rib Shack offered an opportunity to relive some of Atlanta's rich history, savor outstanding ribs, and experience the down-home hospitality of the Taylor-Clements family. For me, that was a winning combination.

DINING:

DEACON BURTON'S SOUL FOOD

Location: 1029 Edgewood Ave, NE
Telephone: (404) 658-9452
Proprietor: Lenn Storey
Dress: Casual/Classy
Menu: Soul Food
Price: Very Modest
Status: **Closed**

Comments: Deacon Burton's Soul Food was a cozy, no-frills eatery tucked away in a white brick building across from the Inman Park Metro Station. When you walked through the serving lines, you could choose among several trays heaped with fried chicken, fried fish, lima beans, corn bread and banana pudding. Several cooks behind the counter busily kept the trays filled or tended to the old burners in the back. Around noon, the restaurant quickly filled with patrons, mostly members of Atlanta's downtown business community and tourists. The late "Deacon" Lyndell Burton founded this landmark restaurant in 1930, during the Great Depression. Burton moved to Atlanta when he was a young teenager and immediately set out in pursuit of his dream of owning a restaurant. He worked in several Atlanta restaurants and, by the age of 21, was a highly regarded chef. Even after he opened his own place, he continued working full-time in more established mainstream restaurants. A very religious and civic-minded man, he also gave freely to both his church and community. As a result, Burton became affectionately known around town as the "Deacon," and his restaurant became an important anchor in his neighborhood. When Deacon Burton passed away in 1992, ownership of the restaurant transferred to his son, Lenn Storey. A public school teacher, Storey divided his time between running the restaurant and maintaining his day job. His wife Beverly devoted full time to the restaurant, and together they stayed true to the legacy of Deacon Burton. Fried chicken was still the focal point, along with fresh vegetables such as collard greens and lima beans. You could get a full-course meal for less than $5. Deacon Burton's Soul Food consistently was acknowledged as the city's best soul-food restaurant by numerous publications.

DINING:

PASCHAL'S HOTEL AND RESTAURANT

Location: 830 Martin Luther King Jr., Blvd
Telephone: (404) 577-3150
Proprietor: James and Ronald Paschal
Dress: Classy
Menu: Southern/Continental
Price: Modest
Status: **Closed**

Comments: The Paschal brothers founded this hotel and restaurant in 1947, and Atlanta's African American have viewed it with pride ever since. The hotel's coffee shop, restaurant, and banquet facilities historically were favorite meeting places for the city's business, civic and political leaders. The late Reverend Dr. Martin Luther King, Jr. held many strategy sessions here while directing the civil rights movement. Former United Nations Ambassador Andrew Young, former Mayor Maynard Jackson, the Reverend Jesse Jackson, Congressman John Lewis, activist and former Georgia State Senator Julian Bond, Senator Ted Kennedy and activist Stokley Carmichael were just a few who conferred at the Paschal's Hotel with Dr. King. I ate here during and after my college days. While many things change, you could always count on this restaurant to provide down-home, Southern-style cooking in an elegant setting. The restaurant was long renowned for its Southern fried chicken. Diners would have it with rice and gravy, collards, and fresh dinner rolls, and were never disappointed. Other highlights included broiled lobster, fried or broiled ocean perch, charbroiled steaks, smothered pork chops, sautéed calf's liver and onions, and a chef's salad bowl. The Paschal brothers' original establishment was a small eatery, seating about 30. In 1959, they constructed a large upscale restaurant. La Carousel followed that same year, and the hotel opened in 1960. The main dining room had a capacity of 150. Paschal's two banquet rooms, the Matador and the Sherwood, seated 250 and 180, respectively. Reservations were encouraged for parties of seven or more. During holidays and major events such as homecomings and graduations in the Atlanta University complex, it was best to get there early! One of the few African American-owned hotels in the country, Paschal's was a must-visit during any visit to Atlanta.

Epilogue: Due to the declining health of the late Robert Paschal, the Hotel and Restaurant were sold to Clark-Atlanta University in 1996. His surviving brother, James, and Atlanta real estate baron Herman Russell opened a new restaurant in 2002 that honors the legacy of this historic hotel and restaurant. See page 33.

Hall of Memories, Jackson, MS Jackson, Mississippi

JAZZ/BLUES/REGGAE:

930 Blues Café

Location: 930 N Congress St
Telephone: 601-948-3344
Clientele: Young/Mature Adult
Format: Mississippi Delta Blues
Calendar: Live Entertainment Mon - Sat
Cover/Minimum: Yes/No
Dress: Casual/Classy
Status: **Closed**
www.jesdablues.com

Comments: The 930 Blues Café has emerged as Jackson's most important and consistent blues club since its opening in 2002. Owner Isaac K. Byrd Jr. is a celebrated Jackson, MS, attorney, entrepreneur, philanthropist and Hall of Fame inductee of his beloved Tugaloo College. Whether in winning landmark legal cases or supporting the arts locally and state wide, he approaches everything with "old school" passion. An avid blues aficionado, his vision for the café was twofold: 1. Create a consistent venue for local and touring blues artists and 2. Create an ambiance that is authentic to the Mississippi Delta. He accomplished the latter by citing the club on historic Congress

Street in a picturesque Victorian home built in 1903, by importing early 1900s artifacts from his family as part of the club's décor. The authentic pinewood floor was restored from the demolition of an old church. Photographs depicting Mississippi Delta scenes line the walls. Patrons navigate their way from the first floor restaurant to the second floor music room by following Delta road signs up the stairs. As the name of their website suggests, the 930 Blues Café is all blues, all the time.

Hall of Memories: North Carolina Triangle, Durham

DINING:

Dillard's Bar-B-Q

Location: 3921 Fayetteville Street, Durham, NC
Telephone: 919-544-1587
Proprietor: The Dillard Family
Dress: Casual/Classy
Menu: Southern
Price: Very Modest
Hours: Mon – Sat 7:00 AM – 9:00 PM (10:00 PM Sat)
Status: **Closed**
www.dillardsbarbq.com

Comments: Dillard's is the Triangle's landmark soul-food restaurant. Founded in 1953 by the late Sam Dillard, it has remained one of the favorite places to eat for generations of area residents. The restaurant is located less than three miles from the North Carolina Central University campus. The building has an attractive yellow wood and beige brick façade. The interior includes a waiting room with a serving counter decorated in white-and-black tile, a display case filled with fresh vegetables and entrees, and a long green formica and white vinyl bench for take-out customers. The right side of the restaurant features a main dining room accented with beige brick and white walls, hanging plants, and pennants representing area Atlantic Coast Conference Schools and historically black colleges. The most requested entrees are the barbecue beef and pork, slow-cooked for three hours over a gas furnace. The sauce is a blend of vinegar, mustard, tomato sauce honey, and crushed red peppers. Other popular entrees include chitterlings with some of the vegetables from the garden, such as steamed cabbage, collard greens, fried okra, and candied yams. Nineteen different sandwiches are offered, including trout, croaker, and spot. The desserts are an appetizing selection of blackberry, blueberry, and apple cobblers, sweet potato pie, and banana pudding. Duke University, the University of North Carolina, and several labs at the Research Triangle Park are among their numerous catering clients. Dillard's Barbecue Sauce is sold over the counter and at several local food stores. The Dillards also maintain a concession stand at the Durham Athletic Park, home of the Durham Bulls baseball team. Sam Dillard's sons, Allen Sr., Edsal, James, and Kelly, along with grandson Allen Jr. are all actively involved in keeping the family's restaurant tradition alive. Stop by and experience one of the Triangle's social and culinary institutions. The food is surpassed only by the down-home ambiance that seems to come hand in hand with such landmark institutions throughout the Southeast.

Hall of Memories: MEMPHIS, TN

JAZZ/BLUES/REGGAE:

Green's Lounge

Location: 2090 East Person Avenue
Telephone: 901-274-9802
Clientele: Mature Adult
Format: Blues
Calendar: Live Entertainment Fri – Sat
Cover/Minimum: Yes/No
Dress: Casual/Classy
Status: **Closed**

Comments: Rose Green operated this traditional blues juke joint for more than 20 years. In January 1994, she turned the club over to Betty Suggs, who also knew her way around the blues circuit, having owned a number of places in Memphis as well as the Silver Slipper in Clarksdale, Mississippi. Green's Lounge was short on pomp and circumstance but heavy, oh so heavy, on low-down, hard-hitting, blues, mostly Delta blues. By day, the club took on the characteristics of an old neighborhood bar. Elderly men played cards, usually Spades or Bid Whist. The jukebox belted out Little Milton tunes, "Struggling Lady" and "Catch You On The Way Back Down". On weekend evenings, the club became transformed, resembling the juke joint recreated in Steven Spielberg's The Color Purple, alive and festive. Willie Roy Sander and the Fieldstones rocked the house for more than two decades, belting out Delta blues steeped in Memphis tradition. Big Joe and the Dynaflows once surprised the folks at Green's Lounge by dropping in to "jump" the house while in town for an engagement at B. B. King's. Regular patrons at Green's Lounge ranged from old faithfuls who had lived in the neighborhood for years, dressed in bell-bottom pants or plaids, to folks who drove up in limousines, sporting the latest fashions in evening wear. Rich or poor, white or black, they all had one thing in common. They wanted to hear and experience the blues as it was sung and performed at juke joints throughout the Delta and in Memphis by legendary blues artists during the early Twentieth Century. Rose Green was coaxed out of retirement to bring back another feature of the club from years past, down-home cooking that yielded soulful staples such as chitterlings, ham hocks, turnips, and black-eyed peas. If you were a diehard blues connoisseur, your stay in Memphis would not have been complete without stepping back in time and jamming at Green's Lounge.

Epilogue: Green's Lounge was destroyed by fire in 1997. Legendary blues artist Will Roy Sanders, "the Lost Living Bluesman" and leader of the Fieldstones, passed away on February 16th, 2010.

JAZZ/BLUES/REGGAE:

New Club Paradise

Location: 645 George Avenue
Telephone: 901-947-7144
Clientele: Young/Mature Adult
Format: Blues/R&B
Calendar: Live Entertainment Varied
Cover/Minimum: Yes/No
Dress: Casual/Classy
Status: **Closed**

Comments: The late "Sunbeam" Andrew Mitchell was both a musician and an entrepreneur. He was at the core of African American life in Memphis during the late 1960s. Under the helm of Mitchell, Club Paradise set the standard for blues, jazz, and R&B in the region at a time when no other entertainment venues existed for African Americans there. During peak periods, Club Paradise drew standing room-only crowds five nights a week. This was partly attributed to a list of acts that virtually chronicled the evolution of blues, jazz, and R&B in the United States; performers included the Count Basie Band, Cab Calloway, Muddy Waters, Howlin' Wolf (Chester Arthur Burnett), James Brown, Jackie Wilson, and Etta James. Paul Jordon took over the club and renamed it New Club

Paradise in 1985. He was fiercely dedicated to keeping the legacy of this historic establishment alive. The management spent more than a million dollars on renovations to achieve that objective. The club's plain façade completely concealed the sleek and attractive décor inside. After it reopened in 1985, the club was host to acts such as Freddie Jackson, Melba Moore, Denise LaSalle, Tyronne Davis, and the O'Jays. Jordan had hoped to reestablish New Club Paradise as a top entertainment center for Memphis residents and visitors.

JAZZ/BLUES/REGGAE:

The North End

Location: 346 North Main Street
Telephone: 901-526-0319
Clientele: Young/Mature Adult
Format: Blues/Jazz
Calendar: Live Entertainment Varied
Cover/Minimum: Yes/No
Dress: Casual/Classy
Status: **Closed**

Comments: The North End was a large and airy establishment located near the Pyramid complex in the downtown area. It had the feel of a college bistro, a description borne out by North End's immense popularity among Memphis State students and young Memphis professionals. North End had high ceilings and a décor accentuated by an interesting assortment of memorabilia on the walls, such as old Coca Cola and gas station signs. The club seated 120, while the patio accommodated another 100 patrons. On Wednesdays, Roco's Band performed an eclectic blend of music that ranged from bluegrass to traditional jazz. The Wilson Reid Band played contemporary country music each Saturday night. Sid Selvidge packed the house with Delta blues each Friday, while Jungle Dust played fusion jazz on Sundays. For most shows, you had to arrive by 9:30 PM to get your choice of seats for the first set of the evening, which began at 10:00 PM. There were three sets, each running about 45 minutes. While most patrons came to hear jazz and blues, many just came for North End's cuisine, a menu that included the best marinated chicken sandwich in town and a hot fudge concoction topped with French vanilla ice cream and whipped cream that was something to die for. The restaurant was open daily for lunch and dinner. North End also offered the largest imported beer selection in the city. Owner Jake Schorr was a director of the Memphis Queen lines and also owned a fleet of horse-drawn carriages. His diverse business interests translated into a windfall for patrons of the North End; they could hear some outstanding local blues and jazz acts, have a great meal, arrange a tour of the city by carriage, and set up a riverboat cruise on one of the Memphis Queen line's blues excursions to Tunica, Mississippi, all in one stop.

Epilogue: You can still get Jake Schorr's decadent desserts like his hot fudge pie at Westy's, a restaurant he co-owns in the Pinch District of the city.

JAZZ/BLUES/REGGAE:

Willie Mitchell's Rhythm and Blues Club

Location: 326 Beale Street
Telephone: 901-523-7444
Clientele: Young/Mature Adult
Format: Blues/R&B
Calendar: Live Entertainment Varied
Cover/Minimum: Yes/No
Dress: Casual/Classy
Status: **Closed**

Comments: In 1994, Willie Mitchell's Rhythm & Blues Club was one of the newest additions to the Beale Street entertainment scene. Gold and Platinum albums of gospel and R&B star Al Green lined the walls at the entrance, a testament to the creative achievements of the club's namesake, composer and arranger Willie Mitchell. A hardwood bar inlaid with green-and-white tile and a large hardwood dance floor highlighted the first room. A second room, lined with scores of photos depicting legendary R&B stars, was used as a meeting and conference room. An outdoor patio decorated with white wrought-iron patio furniture also was used as an entertainment venue. The club's capacity was 250. Bobby Rush and the Hi Rhythm Band with Teenie Hodges and the Hodges Brothers were among the first touring acts to play the club. Local star Preston Shannon and the Preston Shannon Band were regularly featured. Trumpeter and composer Willie Mitchell played the room in July 1994, his first performance in the United States in 25 years. The club's goal was to feature touring acts monthly as well as an occasional appearance by Mitchell. Local promoter Bob Winbush hosted a talent search, "Stairway to the Stars," each Wednesday night. Yvonne Mitchell founded the club in March 1994. She and her sister Lorraine had co-managed R&B entertainer Ann Peebles for a number of years. Yvonne Mitchell also was something of a "lady Friday" for Royal Record Studios (formerly Hi Records) during the early 1970s, providing assistance to her father, Willie Mitchell in a wide range of duties. Willie Mitchell's Rhythm & Blues Club was very much a family affair with Willie Mitchell's grandchildren, Archie, Donna and Lawrence actively involved in the business. The menu included entrees such as roast prime rib, grilled shrimp, smothered chicken, red beans & rice and a catch of the day. Their desserts included homemade cobblers, coconut and pecan pies.

Epilogue: Willie Mitchell, venerable R&B pioneer and record producer, passed away in Memphis on January 5, 2010. He received the Grammy Foundation's Lifetime Achievement Award in 2008. His grandson Lawrence took over the day-to-day operations of Mitchell's Royal Studios, located on Willie Mitchell Boulevard, during his later years. It was from this studio that he shaped the careers of legendary R&B artists such as Al Green, OV Wright, Ann Peebles and Otis Clay.

DINING:

Neely's Bar-B-Que

Location: 670 Jefferson Blvd.
Telephone: 901-521-9798
Proprietor: Patrick and Tony Neely
Dress: Casual/Classy
Menu: Barbecue
Price: Modest
Status: **Closed**

Comments: Neely's Bar-B-Que is more than a rib house. It's an attractive, spacious restaurant just minutes from downtown Memphis. The menu features a smorgasbord of delights such as heaping sandwiches of sliced/chopped beef and pork as well as California beef links, whole slabs of beef and pork as well as California beef links, whole slabs of beef and pork ribs, and delicious homemade desserts made from Mom's (Lorine Neely's) secret recipes, prepared under her personal supervision. According to Patrick Neely, the keys to their barbecue's popularity are slow-cooking over their specially designed ovens and their sauce, made from 20 different ingredients and sold in grocery stores all over Memphis and outlying Shelby County. The other keys to their to their restaurant's success are their outstanding cole slaw, baked beans, and barbecue spaghetti. The Neely brothers' uncle, Jim Neely, owns Neely's Interstate Bar-B-Que. That's where Patrick and Tony got their initial experience before leaving to undergo management training with the McDonalds Corporation. While working for McDonalds, they gained both the extra experience and the extra confidence they needed to succeed in their initial restaurant venture. They opened a second restaurant in east Memphis in October 1992, Neely's Bar-B-Que (East) and 5700 Mt. Moriah Road. The Neely brothers like to serve as mentors for other young African Americans, and Patrick is helping one of their employees realize his dream of owning his own restaurant. Catering is a large part of their enterprise. The restaurant hosted the cocktail party for the judges of the 1994 Memphis in May Barbecue Festival, and the brothers were invited by Vice President Al Gore to serve barbecue for a party that he gave in the fall of 1994. NBC Bank has featured Neely's Bar-B-Que in their annual report as one of the top Memphis businesses. The Neely's have undergone enormous success since my first visit in 1994. Pat and Gina Neely have become media stars thanks to their Food Network cooking show, Down Home with the Neely's. Drop by and see why Memphis natives consider this restaurant among their favorites.

Epilogue: Pat & Gina announced the closing of their Memphis restaurants in October, 2012. MyFoxmemphis.com reported the official closings on 2 July, 2013. The Neely couple continue to enjoy enormous success on cable T.V. with their cooking show. Jim Neely and his Interstate Bar-B-Que restaurant still carry the torch as the founder of the Neely tradition in fine barbecue.

DINING:

Melanie's & The Leach Family Restaurant
Location: 1070 N. Watkins St
Telephone: 901-278-0751
Proprietor: Jimmie Mae Cotton-Leach and the Leach Family
Dress: Casual
Menu: Soul Food
Price: Modest
Status: **Closed**

Comments: Jimmie Mae Cotton-Leach always enjoyed cooking and collecting recipes, and she has cooked for her church most of her life. When visiting evangelists came to town in the 1960s, the Leach family housed and fed them, and on Sundays, all the neighbors would come over to eat. The idea of opening a family restaurant came as an inspiration. Melanie's is located in a neighborhood that once was called the mid-town area. It has a serving line, but is primarily geared towards take-out orders. The tiny eatery seats about 30 in small booths adorned with blue-and-white tablecloths. The most-requested entrees are fried catfish, served only on Fridays, and fried chicken, served Wednesdays and Saturdays. Both are cooked to a golden brown using special seasonings and spices developed by Mrs. Cotton-Leach. The secret to her chitterlings is that she pot-boils them, washes them again, and then adds yet another of her special seasonings. Other items from the menu include greens, ham hocks, and yams. The restaurant is also well known for delicious lemon cake, peach cobbler, and banana pudding. Melanie's caters for church gatherings, weddings and local business events. Their cakes are so popular that the Leach family was able to sponsor bake sales to help lay the foundation for their church, True Gospel Church of God and Christ. They give additional support to the local community by providing meals on request to the Greater Movement Homeless Shelter and the Salvation Army. Melanie's is an excellent choice for down-home cooking.

Hall of Memories: NEW ORLEANS, LA

JAZZ/BLUES/REGGAE:

Maxwell's Toulouse Cabaret

Location: 615 Toulouse Street
Telephone: 504-523-4207
Clientele: Young/Mature Adult
Format: Jazz
Calendar: Live Entertainment Varied
Cover/Minimum: Yes (includes 1 drink)/No
Dress: Casual/Classy
Status: **Closed**

Comments: Maxwell's Toulouse Cabaret captured the attention the moment you walked in. The little bar in front was bursting with color. The multicolored Second Line umbrellas that are very much a feature of Mardi Gras parades and jazz funerals hung from the rafters. Posters depicting some of the city's jazz legends vied for your attention. A musical family tree showed the origins of African American music and its influence on American music in general. The grand cabaret was as subtle as the entrance was not. Cocktail tables were comfortably arranged on four levels that sloped down towards the stage. That's where your attention was riveted, to the music — traditional New Orleans jazz. New Orleans legends that performed here included Harry Connick, Sr., the Sounds of New Orleans featuring Rene Netto, and the New Orleans Kings of Rhythm. Every set normally ended in a New Orleans traditional dance, the Second Line. There was not a bad seat in the house.

JAZZ/BLUES/REGGAE:

New Showcase Lounge

Location: 1915 North Broad Street
Telephone: 504-945-5612
Clientele: Young/Mature Adult
Format: Jazz/Blues/R&B
Calendar: Live Entertainment Varied
Cover/Minimum: Yes / No
Dress: Casual/Classy
Status: **Closed**

Comments: This was the quintessential neighborhood bar; New Orleans style, but rather on the tough side. It was a local joint whose popularity expanded well beyond its own environs. New Showcase Lounge throbbed and flowed. Outside the quaint and homey building, you would find cars parked everywhere – along the streets, on the meridians – a sure sign that this was a happening place. Inside, there was a piano-shaped bar with a white-brick facade and bar stools with red vinyl cushions. Red light rhythmically traced the bar's outline overhead. Small cocktail tables bedecked in red crammed the main room opposite the bar. A sign in the corner read "all you can eat buffet: $6.00." The Snap Bean Band led by drummer Walter Payton and featuring the diminutive dynamo Sharon Martin packed them in every Sunday night. Playing a range of music from straight ahead jazz to Oleta Adams to traditional blues, they found an appreciative audience in a house that took you back to the Crescent City as it was during the 1960s. Patrons spontaneously sang along, danced in the aisles, or laughed approvingly when vocalist Sharon Martin would coax a local regular called "O.C." on stage. To everyone's delight, he would do the "James Brown slide" as the band rocked to Brown's "I Feel Good."

JAZZ/BLUES/REGGAE:

Old Absinthe House Bar

Location: 400 Bourbon Street
Telephone: 504-525-8108
Clientele: Young/Mature Adult
Format: Blues
Calendar: Live Entertainment Varied
Cover/Minimum: No/Yes (1 drink)
Dress: Casual/Classy
Status: **Closed**

Comments: Legend has it that the privateer Jean LaFitte considered this his personal watering hole when he plied the waters of the Caribbean off the Louisiana Gulf Coast. During my first visit in 1991, the club manager, Larry Geer, related the story that LaFitte would bring his cargo into the city and advertise his wares on a chalkboard at the bar. When absinthe was brought into New Orleans by the French during the 1830s, a number of establishments that sold the drug sprang up across the city, all calling themselves Absinthe House. There was yet another Absinthe House, containing one of the French Quarter's most famous restaurants and bearing a National Historic Register Market, one block up from this location. From the late 1950s through the early 1980s, the Old Absinthe House Bar featured everything from popular plays to reggae. In 1983, the bar began featuring New Orleans blues man Bryan Lee and the Jump Street Five. Their popularity grew to the point that they were virtually synonymous with Old Absinthe House. Playing a range of blues from country to jump to urban, they provided a compelling reason to drop in and sample the action. Lee would later record two live CDs at this venerable establishment, "Bryan Lee Live at the Old Absinthe House Bar: Friday Night CD" and "Bryan Lee Live at the Old Absinthe House Bar, vol. 2: Saturday CD." The club was a narrow little room with tables scattered throughout. Dollar bills lined the walls, dating back to World War II, when the young men of the neighborhood would post dollar bills as talismans to ensure their safe return from the war. The All Purpose Blues band alternated a couple of nights each week. The club was featured in Rolling Stone magazine, in all of the city's local publications and guides, as well as in numerous European travel guides. Getting there early assured a seat nearest the band.

Epilogue: The Old Absinthe House, a "cousin institution," is located at 240 Bourbon Street. It was founded in the early 1800s and houses the original bar from the now defunct Old Absinthe House Bar. The marble bar, paintings and cash register were hidden when the Old Absinthe House doors were shuttered by federal marshals during Prohibition. That hiding place was the Old Absinthe Bar. The artifacts were returned to their original home, Old Absinthe House, in 2004.

DINING:

Olivier's The Creole Restaurant

Location: 204 Decatur Street
Telephone: 504-525-7734
Proprietor: Armand Olivier, Jr.
Dress: Classy
Menu: Creole Cuisine
Price: Moderate
Status: **Closed**
URL: www.olivierscreole.com

Comments: Olivier's is an elegant Creole restaurant located across the street from the House of Blues in the French Quarter. The restaurant's décor and theme is turn-of-the-century New Orleans: soft, earthy pastels dominated by subtle yellow and brick, regal mahogany and oak fixtures, and artwork celebrating the contributions of African Americans to the city's cultural life. The menu features classic Creole dishes such as étoufées, jambalaya, and gumbo. Their Creole rabbit is both a succulent entree and a testament to Armand Oliver, Jr and his wife, Cheryl Gaudet Olivier's great grandmother, the late Jean Doublelet Gaudet. Her Creole rabbit was the family's traditional Sunday meal during the Great Depression, when rabbit meat was a much of a staple as chicken is today. Olivier uses grandmother's special recipe to prepare a meal that has become one of the restaurant's trademarks. The rabbit is oven-braised at a low temperature for an hour. Then it is stewed another two hours in a hearty roux. The dish is served with rice pilaf or oyster dressing and covered with more of its special roux. Another item from the menu is a fantastic seafood smorgasbord called Tasters Platter. It includes seafood delicacies such as deep-fried filets, shrimp, oysters, Creole gumbo, stuffed crab and salad. The music often heared in the background is traditional New Orleans jazz played by the legendary clarinetist Sydney Bechet, a pioneer in bringing jazz to an international audience.

His great-grandnephew Armand Olivier III and Terrence Bechet are the restaurant's managers. You also will find paintings by Ron Bechet, an ultra-realist and Terrence's brother, hanging in the dining room. Armand Jr. and his brother Milton lend their expertise behind the scenes, and Armand Jr.'s wife Cheryl, the matriarch of the restaurant, oversees the kitchen. Don't miss an opportunity to stop by and sample some of their outstanding cuisine and good old-fashioned Southern hospitality.

Oliver's "Three Gumbo Sampler" (Seafood, File and Creole)

Hall of Memories: WASHINGTON DC (Metropolitan Area)

DINING:

B. Smith's at Union Station

LOCATION: 50 Massachusetts Avenue NE
TELEPHONE: (202) 289-6188
PROPRIETOR: Dan Gasby & B. Smith
DRESS: Casual / Classy
MENU: Cajun, Creole and Southern Cuisine
PRICE: Moderate/Expensive
Status: **Closed**
URL: www.bsmith.com

Comments: Barbara "B" Smith is the penultimate entrepreneur. Her success as a model, media star, lifestyle consultant and restaurateur, has propelled her into a national and international brand. The first B. Smith restaurant was established in 1986. B. Smith could not have chosen a more historic venue for her foray into Washington DC. The restaurant was initially the "Presidential Suite" at Union Station, a place where a President and his First Lady could retire away from the pressing crowds. The exquisite suite was opened to the public in the mid-1980s, housing the Adirondacks Restaurant until 1992. B

Smith transformed the restaurant to her vision when she opened this restaurant in 1994. Dan Gasby, husband, business partner and soul mate, manages the day-to day operations of their three restaurants, located in Times Square (New York), Union Station (Washington DC) and Sag Harbor (Long Island, NY). Upon meeting him, he immediately impressed me as the perfect host. Amazingly, I was greeted affably upon entering and treated as though we had known each for years. Like its more northern counterparts, B. Smith's at Union Station is chic and sophisticated. I tried the bayou catfish, a succulent dish with sautéed crawfish, andouille sausage and Dijon sauce, garnished with a hint of collards, green beans and carrots and served atop a bed of saffron rice.

A Washington DC must visit since it's opening in 1994; you should include this restaurant on your itinerary because of the excellent food, beautiful décor, and, of course, the opportunity to break bread with Washington DC "movers and shakers." Upon leaving the restaurant, I said goodbye to Mr. Gasby and asked him to say hello to a mutual friend in New York just as Congressman Alcee Hastings of Florida walked over and introduced himself, flashing his trademark smile. Whether it's President Barack Obama and First Lady Michelle, rock star or movie mogul, this definitely is a place to "see and be seen."

Epilogue: The Owners are evaluating other locations in the Washington Metro area for a Grand Re-opening

JAZZ/BLUES/REGGAE:

KING OF FRANCE TAVERN

LOCATION: 16 Church Circle (Annapolis, MD)
TELEPHONE: (301) 261-2206 / (410) 269-0990
CLIENTELE: Mature Adult
FORMAT: Jazz
CALENDAR: Live Performances Fri-Sun
COVER/MINIMUM: No/Yes
DRESS: Casual/Classy
Status: **Closed**

COMMENTS: The King of France Tavern was located in the historic Maryland Inn, one of the landmarks of Annapolis, MD. The Inn dates back to the 18th century. Hardback chairs, tables fashioned from the tops of beer barrels and cobblestone floors all combine to permeate the senses with the feel of history and tradition. The King of France Tavern along with the Maryland Inn was restored to their original grandeur in the mid '70s. That just about corresponds to the time when the owners of the tavern transformed it into one of the area's premier jazz spots. This rectangular-shaped, low-lit room was tailor-made for the art. The late Charlie Byrd was the first act to perform here, becoming a monthly staple. He would always return to rave reviews between his rigorous national and international touring schedule. Many of the legends of jazz stopped in to jam when they were in the area. Dave Brubeck and the Count Basie Orchestra dropped in within days of each other during an October 1993 slate. A tour of the Naval Academy campus, a visit to the beautiful Annapolis harbor, and an evening at the Tavern provide special memories for anyone who experienced the King of France Tavern.

JAZZ/BLUES/REGGAE:

One Step Down

LOCATION: 2517 Pennsylvania Ave. N.W.
TELEPHONE: (202) 331-8863
CLIENTELE: Mature Adult
FORMAT: Jazz
CALENDAR: Live Performances Thur-Mon
COVER/MINIMUM: No/Yes
DRESS: Casual/Classy
Status: **Closed**
URL: www.onestepdown.com

COMMENTS: One Step Down was an old Georgetown establishment that kept the faith and held true to its devotion to jazz. Joe Cohen opened the club in 1963. When I spoke with him during my first visit in 1993, Cohen recounted that he started with a collection of jazz cuts offered to his patrons on a juke box sound system. The juke box remained there and the cuts grew into an enormous collection of jazz classics. One Step Down began featuring live jazz during the mid-1970s. Notables such as Ellis Marsalis, Curtis Fuller, Chet Baker and Barry Harris have performed here. Often, jazz greats who were in town performing at larger venues would drop in for a jam session. The late, great Dizzy Gillespie would often come in just to shoot the breeze and relax. Dick Webster sometimes sent students from his Georgetown University Jazz Class here to do an essay on some of the artists who were performing. Once a month, the University of Maryland conducted a jazz workshop here.

As you walked into One Step Down, you would notice a dimly lit room that was small, but chock full of character and tradition. The collection of old "axes" (horns) that hung along the walls added to this feeling, and so did the posters of jazz festivals long past. One Step down was an historic venue in The Nation's Capital.

Epilogue: Owner and founder Joe Cohen passed away in the Fall of 1997. Catherine Stuart, a family friend, ran the club until the Fall of 2000, whereupon it closed. Their website is still active. A succinct note at the top of the page reads "Dear friends and patrons, I regret to inform you but the One Step Down is now closed. The building was sold to a developer and will be turned into apartments."

JAZZ/BLUES/REGGAE:

PIER 7

LOCATION: 650 Water St. N.W.
TELEPHONE: (202) 554-2500
CLIENTELE: Young/Mature Adult
FORMAT: R&B/Jazz
CALENDAR: Live Performances Tues-Sat
COVER/MINIMUM: No/Yes
DRESS: Classy
Status: CLOSED

COMMENTS: Pier 7 was founded in 1972. It has always had a jazz venue that features a house band. Elite, a classical jazz trio, has been the band of choice since 1987. The name of this establishment gives one a hint of what you'll find here. It's a waterfront hideaway that has been popular among D.C. power brokers for a number of years. While the band is well versed in the classical jazz idiom, what the customers prefer most is the opportunity to dance to the rhythms of yesterday.

JAZZ/BLUES/REGGAE:

Tornado Alley

LOCATION: 11319 Elkin Street, Wheaton, MD
TELEPHONE: (301) 929-0795
CLIENTELE: Mature Adult
FORMAT: Blues / Zydeco
CALENDAR: Live Performances Nightly
COVER/MINIMUM: Yes/No
DRESS: Casual/Classy
Status: **Closed**

Comments: Marc Gretschel opened Tornado Alley in January, 1992. It had a short but incredible run over a two year period. It arguably was one of the hottest blues juke joints on the Mid Atlantic coast. Junior Wells, the Nighthawks, Charlie Musselwhite, James Cotton, Chicago blues guitarist Luther Allison, Zydeco pioneers Roy Carrier and the Nightrockers were just a few of the blues and zydeco stars that played the club. Tornado Alley had a meteoric rise, but could not survive the bad publicity surrounding a tragic act of violence just a block away. Gretschel closed Tornado Alley shortly afterwards, packed up his bags and reopened his enormously popular "Twist & Shout" club in Bethesda, MD. It was the scene of memorable zydeco performances by regional and national acts, immortalized by Mary Chapin Carpenter in her 1992 Grammy winning song, "Down at the Twist and Shout." The Twist & Shout closed its doors in 1998.

Epilogue: Marc Gretschel remains active in the Washington, DC area, organizing benefits for great causes such as New Orleans Katrina relief efforts. DC natives anxiously await his next blues / zydeco venue.

JAZZ/BLUES/REGGAE:

Utopia Bar & Grill

LOCATION: 1418 U Street, NW
TELEPHONE: (202) 483-7669
CLIENTELE: Young/Mature Adult
FORMAT: Blues, Jazz
CALENDAR: Live Performances Tues-Sun
COVER/MINIMUM: Yes/Yes
DRESS: Casual/Classy
URL: www.utopiaindc.com
Status: CLOSED

Comments: Jamal Sahri opened Utopia Bar & Grill in 1992. It since has gained a very large following among DC jazz fans and art lovers. The décor is as appealing as the entertainment. An aspiring artist, Sahri's original oil paintings are displayed around the room, creating the feel and ambiance of a Mediterranean café.

Utopia's has a rated capacity of 100 patrons. Their restaurant occupies one half of the space, the bar and small tables line the walls of a separate space where the bands set up shop near the entrance. The crowd begins to build as the evening progresses. By the time the band has tuned their instruments, the room is filled with an appreciative audience. Top local jazz acts include The Wayne Wilentz Trio and Jim West (Brazilian Jazz and Blues), The Ed Hahn Quintet and Collector's Edition (classic jazz) and Bill Heid and Paul Piper (jazz and blues).

DINING:

Chef's Table

LOCATION: 4414 Benning Rd N.E.
TELEPHONE: (202) 398-6994
PROPRIETOR: Albert Westbrook
DRESS: Casual/Classy
MENU: Soul Food
PRICE: Modest
Status: **Closed**

COMMENTS: When I visited Chef's Table for the very first time in the early 1990s, I was totally surprised. It may have been one of Washington's best kept secrets. When you drove into their spacious parking lot, you became immediately aware that you were in for a special treat. It was simply one of the most attractive soul food restaurants that you could find anywhere. The Chef's Table was best known for its all-you-can-eat soul food buffet. I tried the potato salad, candied yams, pilaf gumbo, turkey gizzards and cornbread muffin. All were excellent choices. The chitterlings, stuffed turkey rolls and Southern fried chicken were also favorites among the patrons who continued to go back for more. Albert Westbrook opened this establishment in 1972. His experience in the restaurant business went back many years. He had worked with his father, Clarence Westbrook, since the age of 8. The elder Westbrook opened his first restaurant, D.C. Doughnut Shop, during the Great Depression in 1932. He went on to establish a chain of 13 restaurants during the period. His restaurant on U Street was one of the largest in Washington during World War II, seating 150 people and catering to all the stars. Al Westbrook did the family tradition well. This was yet another one of America's historic family enterprises.

Epilogue: Considered a "landmark institution" of Washington DC's Ward 7, the site was purchased in 2009 by Ben Soto, a Washington DC entrepreneur and power broker. He envisions converting the site to retail and residential development, including a sit-down restaurant.

DINING:

Faces

LOCATION: 5625 Georgia Ave. N.W.
TELEPHONE: (202) 291-6085
PROPRIETOR: Donzell Tate
DRESS: Casual/classy
MENU: Soul Food
PRICE: Modest
Status: **Closed**

COMMENTS: In 1994, Faces was one of Washington's oldest African-American owned restaurants and lounges. It originally opened in the early '70s. Donzell Tate became the owner in 1976. This attractive establishment was a favorite meeting place for Washington political, business and educational leaders from its very inception. The décor was simple yet elegant in an understated way. The main dining room was situated on one side of the restaurant and faced the kitchen. A circular bar was located in the center of the room. There also were tables located on the opposite side of the room along with a raised dining area with booths. On weekends, or whenever patrons were in a festive mood, a few of the dining tables were moved aside in order to make room for dancing. Faces had an outstanding menu that featured calf''s liver & onions, a crab cake platter, barbecue ribs and an array of fried fish such as catfish, trout and whiting. Patrons especially favored their fillet of trout, which was mouthwatering. This restaurant was perhaps one of Washington's defining institutions. A visit here was an opportunity to experience the pulse of D.C.

DINING:

JOPLIN'S

LOCATION: 2225 Georgia Ave. N.W.
TELEPHONE: (202) 462-5400
PROPRIETOR: Howard University
DRESS: Casual/Classy
MENU: Soul Food/Continental
PRICE: Moderate
Status: **Closed**

COMMENTS: The Howard Inn was an outstanding establishment situated on the edge of the Howard University campus, founded by Washington DC developer Eddie Murphy. The dining room was called the Harumbee Restaurant. Howard University took over ownership in the early '80s and renamed the hotel's restaurant Joplin's. It was located on the second floor. As you entered Joplin's, soft lights, pastel colors and crystal chandeliers ushered you in. Old standards of rhythm & blues as well as jazz were piped softly over the sound system. An eclectic menu of soulful cuisine and traditional fare awaited you. I tried their southern fried chicken, potato salad and rice—a standard soul food dish that Joplin's did just the right way. Other menu items included Louisiana style catfish, New Orleans gumbo, filet mignon, and whole rainbow trout. Whether you were in DC to take in the sights of the nation's capital or for a Howard University football game, a stop in at Joplin's for dinner and a tour of the Howard campus was just the ticket.

DINING

Levi's North Carolina Barbecue

LOCATION: 5310 Indian Head Hwy N.W., Oxon Hill, MD
TELEPHONE: (301) 567-1700
PROPRIETOR: Levi and Gloria Durham
DRESS: Casual/Classy
MENU: Soul Food/Continental
PRICE: Modest
Status: **Closed**

COMMENTS: Levi and Gloria Durham are originally from Goldsborough, NC. They brought a little bit of the Carolinas to Washington, DC by way of their soul food restaurant. Levi's first taste of entrepreneurship came at the tender age of 20 when he owned and operated a gas station. He and Gloria ventured into the restaurant business in 1989. Levi's had a large and faithful following. It always was best to call ahead and place your order so that you would not have to wait in line. Levi developed quite a reputation—so much so that the late Sen. Edward Kennedy invited him out to do the ribs for an annual 4th of July barbecue. Levi also catered most of former heavyweight champion Riddick Bowe's parties. While his first restaurant was better suited to take out orders, Levi's opened a second restaurant in November 1993 at 1233 Brentwood Rd Northeast. It was spacious enough to accommodate their many appreciative customers in the DC area. Both restaurants offered a tantalizing menu that featured baked fish, fried fish, North Carolina barbecue ribs, soulful veggies and sweet pies. My favorite was the fried fish with potato salad and hush puppies. The North Carolina ribs also were a treat. Levi credited the popularity of the ribs to a special North Carolina vinegar-based sauce developed by Montel Scott Sr. of Goldsborough, NC and slow cooked meat that was prepared fresh daily. Levi Durham, when asked about the key to his success, simply stated, "We open each day at the restaurant with all the employees holding hands in a circle and offering a prayer of thanks."

Epilogue: SOLD

Appendix I

Crescent City Notes

The aftermath of Hurricane Katrina and its destruction along the Gulf Coast, especially in New Orleans, has been much chronicled in print and media. I can vividly recall conversations with my cousins, Thelma Rudison Thomas and Delores Rudison, residents of Gentilly and the 9th Ward, as the storm bore down on New Orleans. "You have to leave, the city has not seen anything like this in our lifetime." They hesitated, reminding me that the city had set aside the Superdome as a shelter of last resort. I called them again, 24 hours before the storm was predicted to make land fall somewhere around Grand Isle. They still were in the city and uncertain whether they would leave. Watching with horror as the storm's path of destruction was shown live; I became very anxious, not knowing whether my cousins had taken my advice. The world watched with disbelief as the levees began to develop cracks, water rising by the inch, then by the foot. As news teams began to show footage of tragic scenes from the Superdome "shelter" and stranded residents on rooftops, my concern for my relatives became even more heightened. It would be days before I was given the fantastic news that Thelma had taken shelter in Baton Rouge, LA. Delores and her family did not stop their car until they reached Houston, TX. Delores recently returned to the city and is making the final repairs to her home on Caffin Avenue in the city's Ninth Ward. Thelma has settled in Baton Rouge but repairs to her Gentilly neighborhood on Mirabeau Avenue continue.

New Orleans residents faced a gut-wrenching choice: Do I stay in my home or take to the highway, bound for some unfamiliar land? Thousands left, yet too many others remained. In retrospect, the city was woefully unprepared to deal with the Katrina's devastation and the flooding that occurred in its aftermath. So was the state and nation. The city continues to reconstitute itself, rising from the ashes like the mythological phoenix; not burned by fire but rising after the water receded.

In the Storm's Wake

Federal, State and local resources mobilized to provide to rescue efforts, disaster assistance and relief for New Orleans citizens and residents throughout the Gulf Coast that were affected by Hurricane Katrina. A cooperative effort by concerned citizens also has resulted in the provision of essential services that are ongoing. Here are just a few:

- Churches in Baton Rouge, New Orleans, throughout the state of Louisiana and America immediately responded to the emergency, providing shelter, food, clothing and financial assistance to Gulf Coast and New Orleans flood victims. Their efforts continue.

- New Orleans Jazz Musicians Brandford Marsalis and Harry Connick, Jr., Ann Marie Wilkins, and Jim Pate founded the Musicians Village, a joint effort with the New Orleans Habitat. The project has resulted in the construction of 75 single family homes and 5 elderly homes in Musician's Village to date. The foundation also is constructing the Ellis Marsalis Music Center on the 8.1 acre site in New Orleans' Lower 9th Ward. The center will serve as a state of the art performance venue, an incubator for teaching and training the next generation of New Orleans musicians and a gathering place for musicians both young and old. www.nolamusiciansvillage.org

- Actor Brad Pitt founded "Make It Right" in 2007, a program to build eco-friendly homes for New Orleans residents displaced by the storm. They have constructed 50 homes thus far and helped 200 families return to the Lower 9th Ward. Their goal is the construction of 100 more homes. www.makeitrightnola.org

- New Orleans native and actor Wendell Pierce is leading an initiative to rebuild homes in Pontchartrain Park, another New Orleans neighborhood that was hard hit by Katrina. Their goal is to obtain 250 abandoned homes from the city, restore them, and sell the homes at reduced prices to returning citizens. So far, 200 families are on the waiting list to purchase. www.pontchartrainpark.org

- The Preservation Resource Center (PRC) of new Orleans, founded in 1974, is dedicated to preserving and restoring historic New Orleans architecture. Their Rebuild Together New Orleans programs has provided assistance to low income families since 1988. After Katrina, their mission expanded to rebuilding and restoring storm damaged homes in an effort to help those who were displaced by Katrina. Their rebuilding efforts focus on the New Orleans neighborhoods of Broadmoor, Esplanade Ridge & Tremé, Faubourg St. Roch, Gentilly, Hollygrove, Holy Cross, and Mid-City. Hundreds of families have been helped so far. The goal of the national arm of Rebuild Together is the restoaration of 1,000 homes throughout the Gulf Coast. www.rebuildingtogether.org, www.rtno.org (Rebuild Together New Orleans).
- Film Actor and Director Spike Lee's HBO Documentaries provide much needed visibility on New Orleans recovery efforts: what happened, what's needed and where to we go from here?
    - *When the Levees Broke: A Requiem in Four Acts, 2006*
    - *If God Is Willing And Da Creek Don't Rise, 2010*
- David Simon and Eric Overmyer co-wrote the hit HBO series The Wire. In April, 2010, they unveiled another HBO blockbuster**,** *Tremé***.** It celebrates New Orleans culture, focusing on the historic Fauborg Tremé section of the city. Even more, the series provides a national spot light on the city by addressing the lives of citizens just after Hurricane Katrina, their efforts to rebuild and beyond. New Orleans natives Wendell Pierce and Phyllis Montana LeBlanc help give the cast a local flavor. So do appearances by New Orleans musicians such as Allen Toussaint, Kermit Ruffin, Troy "Trombone Shorty" Andrews, and "Uncle" Lionel Batiste.

- The New Orleans Saints football team has been a rallying point for New Orleans citizens, invaluable to the morale and welfare of the city. From the owner down to the equipment manager, their dedication to the city from the moment the effects of the storm unfolded has been unwavering. Their Super Bowl Championship in 2010 Other organizations like

Essence Magazine and the National Association of Realtors (NAR) also have demonstrated an enormous commitment to the city by holding their annual festival and conferences here.

What New Orleans Needs

Tourism and more tourism — A partnership at the local, state and federal level to create even more tax-based incentive packages for the creation of jobs and improvements to the city's infrastructure —Levees repaired, reinforced and resistant to Cat 5 Storms—The continued return of native New Orleans citizens from points far and near.

Going Forward

Hope remains. New Orleans citizens, a resilient people, draw upon the resources of faith, courage, and a Crescent City spirit of determination. The population has endured the flood, the recession and the BP oil spill, yet nowhere have I found a city more determined than ever to recover its distinctive flair. After all, there is no city in America quite like New Orleans.

Appendix II

Howard University, Setting Trends in History

1908 – 1930 (Primary Incubator of African American Sororities and Fraternities)

- Alpha Kappa Alpha Sorority, Inc., founded on January 15, 1908 at Howard University.
- Delta Sigma Theta Sorority was founded on January 13, 1913 by twenty-two collegiate women at Howard University.
- National Pan-Hellenic Council (NPHC) was founded in Washington DC on the campus of Howard University on May 10, 1930. Members include Alpha Kappa Alpha, Alpha Phi Alpha, Delta Sigma Theta, Iota Phi Theta, Kappa Alpha Psi, Omega Psi Phi, Phi Beta Sigma, Sigma Gamma Rho, and Zeta Phi Beta.
- Omega Psi Phi Fraternity, Inc. was founded on November 17, 1911 on the campus of Howard University
- Phi Beta Sigma was founded nationally on January 9, 1914 at Howard University,
- Zeta Phi Beta Sorority was founded on January 16, 1920 at Howard University.

1926
Dr. Mordecai Wyatt Johnson becomes Howard University's first African American president

1938
Dr. James M. Nabrit, Howard University's second president, "established at Howard …what is generally considered the first systematic course in civil rights in an American law school." www.howard.edu/explore/history.htm

1940
Benjamin O. Davis, Sr. is promoted to brigadier general, first African American general in the U.S. Army. Former Howard Univ. student and M Street High School graduate.

1950
Howard University professor, Dr. Ralph Bunche, becomes the first African-American to win the Nobel Peace Prize.

1954
Thurgood Marshall wins historic case Brown v. Board of Education of Topeka, landmark case that nullifies the legal basis of segregation in America.

1967
Nominated by President Lyndon B. Johnson, Thurgood Marshall becomes the first African American to serve on the Supreme Court.

1977
President Jimmy Carter appoints Andrew Young as America's ambassador to the United Nations, the first African American to serve the nation in that capacity.

1978
Dr. LaSalle Leffall, Jr. becomes the African-American president of the American Cancer Society.

1979
Dr. LaSalle Leffall, Jr. elected as the first African-American president of the American College of Surgeons.

1989
Former Virginia Governor Douglas Wilder becomes the first African American elected governor of a U.S. state

1998

President Bill Clinton awards Lieutenant General Benjamin O. Davis his fourth star, promotion to the rank of full general.

2001

Shirley Franklin elected mayor of Atlanta, the first female mayor in city history.

Appendix III

New Orleans Itinerary

Photos by Harold Miles

When my friend Cassandra Harris told me that her company was visiting New Orleans for their annual convention, I volunteered to design an itinerary for them. She also agreed to present plaques from me to selected venues and their proprietors. Needless to say, their visit to New Orleans was memorable, even more enhanced by their access to so many great venue owners, chefs, and musicians. If you are planning a trip to any of the cities highlighted in American Blues, Jazz & Soul Food, be sure to take a copy of the book with you to each venue. Don't be bashful; ask for an autograph from any of these great chefs or entrepreneurs. Follow Cassandra's lead; you also could experience a memorable moment with a legend.

Cassandra with Blue Nile Manager Jesse Paige

Cassandra with Bullet and Dorothy @ Bullets's

Cassandra with legendary Kermit Ruffins @ Bullets's

Bullet's with Emile on the Mic

Cassandra takes in a show at Maison Bourbon

Jamil Sharif Quintet @ Maison Bourbon

Cassandra with the Manager, Palm Court Jazz Café

Cassandra with Legendary Pianist Ellis Marsalis at Snug Harbor

Cassandra with Sweet Lorraine's owners Paul & Sherie

Crinkle receives plaque for Vaughn's Lounge

Cassandra with the Queen of Creole Cuisine, Mama Leah Chase, @ Dooky Chase Restaurant

Cassandra with the Staff of Olivier's Creole Restaurant

Cassandra with Owner & Chef Kerry Seaton, Willie Mae's Scotch House

Illustration I

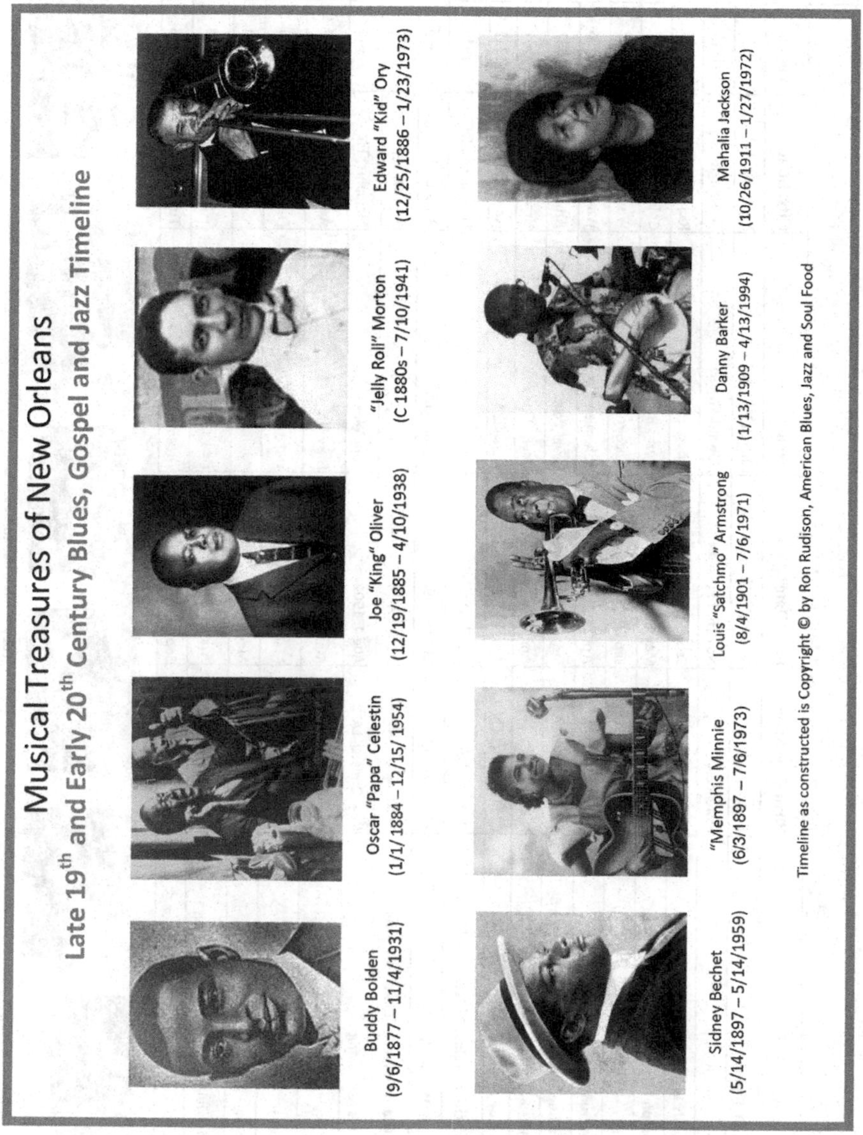

Musical Treasures of New Orleans
Late 19th and Early 20th Century Blues, Gospel and Jazz Timeline
Buddy Bolden
(9/6/1877 – 11/4/1931)
Oscar "Papa" Celestin
(1/1/ 1884 – 12/15/ 1954)
Joe "King" Oliver
(12/19/1885 – 4/10/1938)
"Jelly Roll" Morton
(C 1880s – 7/10/1941)
Edward "Kid" Ory
(12/25/1886 – 1/23/1973)
Sidney Bechet
(5/14/1897 – 5/14/1959)
"Memphis Minnie
(6/3/1897 – 7/6/1973)
Louis "Satchmo" Armstrong
(8/4/1901 – 7/6/1971)
Danny Barker
(1/13/1909 – 4/13/1994)
Mahalia Jackson
(10/26/1911 – 1/27/1972)
Timeline as constructed is Copyright © by Ron Rudison, American Blues, Jazz and Soul Food

Illustration II

American Blues, Jazz & Soul Food A Southeastern Timeline					
Artists	**Birth City, State**	**Birth Date**	**Venues**	**City, State**	**Founded**
Scott Joplin	Texarkana, TX	Nov 24, 1868	Church Park and Auditorium	Memphis, TN	1899
W.C. Handy	Florence, AL	Nov 16, 1873	Howard Theatre	Washington DC	1910
Buddy Bolden	New Orelans, LA	Sep 6, 1877	Hippodrome Theater	Richmond, VA	1914
Joseph "King" Oliver	Aben, LA	May 11, 1885	Scott's Barbecue	Goldsboro, NC	1917
Jelly Roll Morton	New Orelans, LA	Sep 20, 1885	Lincoln Theater	Washington DC	1922
Gertrude Pridgett "Ma Rainey"	Columbus, GA	Apr 26, 1886	Bohemian Caverns	Washington DC	1926
Huddie Wm. Ledbetter, "Lead Belly"	Mooringsport, LA	Jan, 1888	Royal Peacock (old Top Hat Club)	Atlanta, GA	1937
Charley Patton	Northern MS	Apr, 1891	Dooky Chase	New Orleans, LA	1941
Bessie Smith	Chatanooga, TN	Apr 15, 1894	Marsalis Mansion	New Orleans, LA	1943
Lizzie Douglas, "Memphis Minnie"	Algiers, LA	Jun 3, 1897	Florida Avenue Grill	Washington DC	1944
Blind Willie McTell	Thomson, GA	May 5, 1898	Victory Grill	Austin, TX	1945
Edward Kennedy "Duke" Ellington	Washington DC	April 29, 1899	Willie Mae's Scotch House	New Orleans, LA	1945
Louis Armstrong	New Orelans, LA	Aug 4, 1901	Four Way Grill	Memphis, TN	1946
Eddie "Son" House	Coahoma County, MS	Mar 21, 1902	Busy Bee Café	Atlanta, GA	1947
Robert "Barbecue Bob" Hicks	Walnut Grove, GA	March 16, 1905	Dillard's Bar-B-Q	Durham, NC	1953
Robert Johnson	Copiah County, MS	May 8, 1911	Swett's Restaurant	Nashville, TN	1954
McKinley Morganfield, "Muddy Waters"	Issaquena County, MS	Apr 4, 1915	Ben's Chili Bowl	Washington DC	1958
B.B. King	Itta Bena, MS	Sep 16, 1925	Dreamland Bar-B-Que	Tuscaloosa, AL	1958

Illustration III

Illustration IV

American Blues, Jazz & Soul Food

Chart of Origins									
Location	**Europe**	**Africa**	**Middle East**	**India**	**China**	**Indonesia**	**Malaysia**	**Mesoamerica**	**South America**
Foods & Spices	Apples Cabbage (Kazakhstan) Celery Plums (European) Turnip	Blackeye Peas (Cowpea) Celery Coffee Guinea Pepper Melon Oil Palm Okra Watermelon Yam	Asparagus Cantaloupe Carrots Dates Figs Lettuce Olives Onions Pistachios Pomegranate (1) Spinach Walnuts Wheat	Bananas (1) Cinnamon Cucumber Ginger Lemon Mustard Greens Orange Peas Peppercorn Pomegranate (1) Saffron Sugar Cane	Oranges Peaches Pears Plums (Japanese) Rice Soy Beans Tea **Central Asia** Garlic	Mace Nutmeg	Bananas (1)	Avocado Cacao (Cocoa) Common Beans Corn Guava "Hominy Grits" Papaya Pecans Peppers Pumpkin Squash Vanilla Zucchini	Cassava (Yuca) Cashew Nuts Lima Beans Peanuts Pineapples Sweet Potatoes Tomatoes White Potatoes
Other Staples		Frankincense Myrrh (1)	Frankincense Myrrh (1)	Cotton (1)	Silk			Maguey (Agave) Rubber (Costa Rica) (Castilla Elastica) Tobacco	Cotton (1)

Note 1	Archaeological and historical evidence place the origin of some foods, spices and staples in multiple locations dating back to antiquity
Caribbean	Antigua & Barbuda, Bahamas, Barbados, Cuba, Dominica, Dominican Republic, Grenada, Haiti, Jamaica, St. Kitts & Nevis, St. Lucia, St. Vincent & Grenadines, Trinidad & Tobago
Central America	Belize, Costa Rica, El Salvador, Guatemala, Honduras, Nicaragua and Panama.
Mesoamerica	Includes Mexico, Belize, El Salvador, Guatemala, and Honduras. A cultural alignment of countries by Aztec and Mayan heritage and influences
South America	Argentina, Bolivia, Brazil, Chile, Colombia, Ecuador, French Guiana, Guyana, Paraguay, Peru, Suriname, Uruguay and Venezuela
Maguey (Agave)	Portions of the plant were used for food, fibers (ropes) and fermented drinks, today most known for its use to make Tequila and Mezcal
Pecans	The Pecan tree is native to America and Mexico
Sources:	The Cambridge World History of Foods, Atlas of the Native American, USDA Agriculture Research Service, University Websites: Texas A&M, Iowa, etc.

FABULOUS RESOURCE LINKS

American Blues Network

www.americanbluesnetwork.com

"…The American Blues Network is the only 24-hour blues format via satellite…"

Center for Southern Folklore

www.southernfolklore.com

"For nearly 40 years our filmmakers, folklorists and historians have interviewed, recorded, photographed and filmed men and women whose stories, music, foods and crafts represent the diverse traditions and communities of the Memphis/Delta region."

Delta Blues Foundation

www.delta-blues.org

"…a premier, interdisciplinary organization that focuses on the humanities and environmental sciences as they relate to the geography, history, literature, the arts and last but not least the Blues music, Blues history, and Blues culture of the Mississippi Delta."

Downbeat Magazine

www.DownBeat.com

"For 74 years, DownBeat has served as the book of record for the jazz world…"

www.Jazz.com

"Jazz.com offers the most comprehensive and detailed guide to jazz tracks available anywhere"

www.jazzcorner.com

"Features on JazzCorner include: JazzVision - the first and only videosharing site where you can upload and share jazz and blues videos, JazzCorner Jukebox - hundreds of free tunes to surf the net with Jazz always on. News and Calendar - submit your latest news and gigs and events. Speakeasy - one of the busiest bulletin boards and forums for jazz. Podcasts with established and up-and-coming jazz musicians."

Mississippi Blues Trail

www.msbluestrail.org

"…journey into the land that spawned the single most important root source of modern popular music. Whether you're a die-hard blues fan or a casual traveler in search of an interesting trip, this is a source of facts you didn't know, places you've never seen, and you will gain a new appreciation for the area that gave birth to the blues."

Mississippi Musicians Hall of Fame

www.msmusic.org

"The Mississippi Musicians Hall of Fame, whose mission is to inform, educate, and celebrate Mississippi as the birthplace of America's music…"

Southern Food Alliance

www.southernfoodways.com

"…stage symposia on food culture, produce documentary films, publish compendiums of great writing, and—perhaps most importantly—preserve, promote, and chronicle our region's culinary standard bearers. We're talking white tablecloth chefs and fried chicken cooks, barbecue pitmasters and peanut farmers."

Vaucresson's Sausage Company

www.vaucressonsausage.com

1992 Morehouse College graduate Vance Vaucresson represents the 4th generation of a family of 7th Ward New Orleans sausage makers. Local restaurants consider the company's trademark hot sausage *(chaurice)*, Creole smoked sausage, and Andouille as great ingredients for their gumbo, always a New Orleans treat.

"Vaucresson's is the only original food vendor remaining in the Jazz & Heritage Festival. In 1976, famed New York Food Critic Mimi Sheridan, named our Hot Sausage Po-Boy sandwich "Best Food At Fest" during that years "Food Olympics… Since 1899, our family has provided quality sausage products to our community…. Because our products are all-natural and contain no preservatives, and because we want you to enjoy our sausage at its freshest, it is necessary for us to ship it to you via next-day delivery."

BIBLIOGRAPHY

Articles

African Americans in Washington, DC, 1800-1975, by Marya Annette McQuirter, Ph.D.*, capitolcitydc.com/afr.htm.

Ida B. Wells-Barnett and Her Passion for Justice, by Lee D. Baker, April 1996, ldbaker at acpub.duke.edu. Source: Franklin, Vincent P. Living Our Stories, Telling Our Truths: Autobiography and the Making of African American Intellectual Tradition. 1995:

Oxford University Press.

Old Absinthe House Continues To Charm, **article by Stephen McNair, gatewayno.com.**

Books

Autobiography of a People: Three Centuries of African American History Told by Those Who Lived It, Herb Boyd, Doubleday, 2000.

Before the Mayflower: A History of Black America, 6th edition, by Lerone Bennett, Penguin: July 1, 1993.

Father of the Blues: An Autobiography, WC Handy, Da Capo Press, March 22, 1991.

New Orleans Jazz: A Family Album, Al Rose and Edmond Souchon, MD, Louisiana State University Press, 1967.

Nothing But the Blues, Lawrence Cohn, Abbeville Press, 1993.

Profiles of Great African Americans, David Smallwood, Stan West, and Allison Keyes, Publications International Ltd., 1998.

The History of Jazz, 2nd Edition, Ted Gioia, Oxford University Press, 2011.

The World that Made New Orleans: From Spanish Silver to Congo Square, Ned Sublette, Lawrence Hill Books, 2008.

W.C. Handy: The Life and Times of the Man who Made the Blues, David Robertson, Alfred A. Knopf, a Division of Random House, Inc., 2009.

Why New Orleans Matters, Tom Piazza, Harper, Nov. 22, 2005.

Printed in the United States
By Bookmasters